mustsees
CHICAGO

Millennium Park, ©Jill Battaglia/Fotolia.com

Editorial Director	Cynthia Clayton Ochterbeck

mustsees Chicago

Editor	Alison Coupe
Principal Writer	Margaret Littman
Production Manager	Natasha G. George
Cartography	Peter Wrenn
Photo Editor	Yoshimi Kanazawa
Photo Research	Joanne Forrest Smith
Proofreaders	Jonathan P. Gilbert, Rachel Mills
Layout	Alison Rayner, Natasha G. George
Cover & Interior Design	Chris Bell
Contact Us:	Michelin Maps and Guides
	One Parkway South
	Greenville, SC 29615
	USA
	www.michelintravel.com
	michelin.guides@us.michelin.com
	Michelin Maps and Guides
	Hannay House
	39 Clarendon Road
	Watford, Herts WD17 1JA
	UK
	☎(01923) 205 240
	www.ViaMichelin.com
	travelpubsales@uk.michelin.com
Special Sales:	For information regarding bulk sales, customized
	editions and premium sales, please contact
	our Customer Service Departments:
	USA 1-800-432-6277
	UK (01923) 205 240
	Canada 1-800-361-8236

Michelin Apa Publications Ltd

A joint venture between Michelin and Langenscheidt

58 Borough High Street, London SE1 1XF, United Kingdom

© 2009 Michelin Apa Publications Ltd
ISBN 978-1-906261-63-4
Printed: December 2008
Printed and bound: Himmer, Germany

Aerial View of Chicago and Lake Michigan

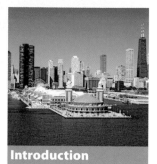

Introduction

**City of Big Shoulders:
Chicago, Illinois**

20

Must Sees

Neighborhoods 22
In the Loop 22
Auditorium Building 22
Former Location of Carson
Pirie Scott & Company 23
Chicago Cultural Center 23
Chicago School of
Architecture 24
Federal Center 24
James R. Thompson Center 24
Richard J. Daley Center 25
Chicago Board of Trade
Building 25
Macy's State St. 26
State Street 26
Along the Boulevard 27
Wrigley Building 27
Tribune Tower 28
InterContinental Chicago 28
Fourth Presbyterian Church 28
Oak Street 30
The Drake Hotel 30
River North 31
Newberry Library 31
Marina City 31
Gold Coast 32
Charnley-Persky House 32
Andersonville 33

Little Saigon 33
Lincoln Square 33
Sulzer Regional Library 34
Old Town 34
Menomonee Street 34
Pilsen 35
Bucktown and Wicker Park 35
Flat Iron Arts Building 35
Bridgeport, Bronzeville
and Chinatown 36
Blues Heaven 36
Illinois Institute of
Technology (IIT) 36
US Cellular Field 36
Lakeview 37
Hyde Park 37
Elijah Muhammad House 37
Landmarks **38**
John Hancock Center 38
Sears Tower 39
Buckingham Fountain 40
Chicago Water Tower and
Pumping Station 42
Wrigley Field 43
Skydeck 43
Museums **44**
Art Institute of Chicago 44
Field Museum of
Natural History 46
Museum of Science
and Industry 48
Shedd Aquarium 49
Adler Planetarium 51
Oriental Institute 53
Chicago History Museum 54
Museum of
Contemporary Art 54
Smart Museum of Art 55
Chinese-American
Museum of Chicago 55
DuSable Museum of African
American History 55
International Museum
of Surgical Science 56

Intuit: The Center for Intuitive
   and Outsider Art   56
Leather Archives and
   Museum   57
McCormick Tribune
   Freedom Museum   57
Mitchell Museum of
   the American Indian   57
Museum of Contemporary
   Photography   57
Museum of Holography   58
National American Italian
   Sports Hall of Fame   58
National Museum of
   Mexican Art   58
Peggy Notebaert Nature
   Museum   59
Polish Museum of America   60
Smith Museum of
   Stained-Glass Windows   60
Spertus Museum   60

Parks and Gardens   **61**
Millennium Park   61
Grant Park   63
Lincoln Park   65
Garfield Park Conservatory   67
Jackson Park   68

Historic Sites   **70**
Graceland Cemetery   70
Robie House   71
Hutchinson Street District   72
Jane Addams Hull-House
   Museum   72
Prairie Avenue
   Historic District   73
Pullman Historic District   74
McCormick Tribune
Bridgehouse and
   Chicago River Museum   76
Richard H. Driehaus Museum   77
Stephen A. Douglas
   Tomb and Memorial   77

Excursions   **78**
Oak Park   78
The Rest of Oak Park's Best   80
North Shore   80
Getting To Know the
   North Shore   81
Morton Arboretum   82
Illinois & Michigan Canal
   National Heritage Corridor   83
Lockport   83
Ottawa   85
Indiana Dunes
   National Lakeshore   85

Must Dos

For Fun   **87**
Outdoor Fun   **91**
For Kids   **93**
Shopping   **102**
Spas   **110**
Nightlife   **113**
Performing Arts   **119**

Must Eat

Restaurants   **124**

Must Stay

Hotels   **139**

Must Know

Star Attractions   **6**
Calendar of Events   **10**
Practical Information   **12**
Index   **154**
Map Index   **160**

TABLE OF CONTENTS

★★★ ATTRACTIONS

Unmissable attractions awarded three stars in this guide include:

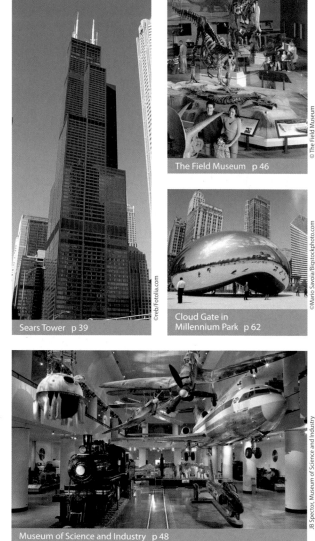

The Field Museum p 46

© The Field Museum

Cloud Gate in
Millennium Park p 62

©Mario Savoia/Bigstockphoto.com

Sears Tower p 39

©reb/Fotolia.com

Museum of Science and Industry p 48

JB Spector, Museum of Science and Industry

©Chicago Architecture Foundation/Anne Evans

Jay Pritzker Pavillion   p 61

©Henryk Sadura/Dreamstime.com

John Hancock Center   p 38

©Jim Jurica/iStockphoto.com

Oak Park   p 78

Auditorium Theatre

Auditorium Building   p 22

©Dave Newman/iStockphoto.com

Art Institute of Chicago   p 44

STAR ATTRACTIONS

7

★★★ ATTRACTIONS

Unmissable sights in Chicago

For more than 75 years people have used the Michelin stars to take the guesswork out of travel. Our star-rating system helps you make the best decision on where to go, what to do, and what to see.

★★★ Absolutely Must See
★★   Really Must See
★   Must See
No Star   See

★★★Three-Stars

Art Institute of Chicago 44
Auditorium Building 22
Carson Pirie Scott & Company 23
Cloud Gate 62
Field Museum of
  Natural History 46
Jay Pritzker Pavilion 61
John Hancock Center 38
The Loop 22
Magnificent Mile 27
Millennium Park Museum
  Campus 64
Museum of Science
  and Industry 48, 95
Oak Park 78
Sears Tower 39
Shedd Aquarium 49, 94

★★Two-Stars

Adler Planetarium 51
Astor Street 32
Baha'i House of Worship
  (Wilmette) 81
BP Bridge 62
Brookfield Zoo 97
Buckingham Fountain 64
Chicago Botanic Garden
  (Glencoe) 81
Chicago Cultural Center 23
Crown Fountain 63
860-880 North Lake
  Shore Drive 30
Federal Center 24
Frank Lloyd Wright Home
  and Studio (Oak Park) 79
Graceland Cemetery 70
Grant Park 63

James R. Thompson Center 24
John Jacob Glessner House 74
Lincoln Park 65
Lincoln Park Zoo 99
Marquette Building 40
Monadnock Building 24
Navy Pier 15, 87, 96
Newberry Library 31
North Shore 80
Oriental Institute 53
Reliance Building 27, 148
Richard J. Daley Center 25
River North 31
Robie House 71
Rookery 24
Tribune Tower 28
Unity Temple (Oak Park) 79
University of Chicago 53
Wrigley Building 27

★One-Star

Bailly Homestead and Chellberg
  Farm and Trail (IN) 86
Charnley-Persky House 32
Chicago Board of Trade Building 25
Chicago Children's Museum 97
Chicago History Museum 54
Chicago Water Tower and
  Pumping Station 42
Drake Hotel, The 30, 140
Dune Succession Trail (IN) 86
Forest Avenue (Oak Park) 79
Fourth Presbyterian Church 28
Frank W. Thomas House (OP) 79
Garfield Park Conservatory 67
Gold Coast 32
Henry B. Clarke House 74
Hutchinson Street District 72

Illinois Institute of Technology 36
Illinois & Michigan Canal NHC 83
Indiana Dunes NLS (IN) 85
InterContinental Chicago 28
Jane Addams
  Hull-House Museum 72
Lincoln Park/DePaul 66
Lockport 83
Lurie Garden 63
Macy's State St. 26
Marina City 31
Menomonee Street 34
Michigan Avenue Bridge 27
Morton Arboretum (Lisle) 82
Mount Baldy (IN) 86
Museum of Contemporary Art 54

Oak Street 30, 103
Old Town 34
Ottawa 85
Peggy Notebaert Nature Museum 59
Pioneer Settlement (Lockport) 84
"Pleasant Home" (Oak Park) 80
Prairie Avenue Historic District 73
Pullman Historic District 74
Riverwalk 22
Smart Museum of Art 55
Smith Museum of
  Stained-Glass Windows 60
State Street 26
Streeterville 30
Water Tower Place 102
West Beach Area (IN) 86
Wrigley Field 43

ACTIVITIES

We recommend every activity in this guide, but the Michelin Man highlights our top picks.

Culture

Intuit: The Center for Intuitive
  and Outsider Art 56
National American Italian Sports
  Hall of Fame 58

Kids

ComedySportz4Kids 101
American Girl Place 100
Children's Museum
  of Immigration 101

Nightlife

Double Door 116
New Checkerboard Lounge for
  Blues 'n' Jazz 115
The Second City 118
The Violet Hour 117
Zanies 118

Recreation

Ice skating at Daley
  Bicentennial Plaza 92
High Tea at the Drake Hotel 30

Restaurants

avec 130
Custom House 127
Green Zebra 127
L20 125
Pizzeria Due 101
Pizzeria Uno 101

Shops

Armitage Avenue 104
Leslie Hindman Auctioneers 108
Southport Avenue 104
The 900 Shops 102

Spas

Asha 110
Kiva Day Spa 111

Theater

Biograph Theater at Victory
  Gardens Theater 90, 123
Steppenwolf Theatre 123

Tours

Architecture Foundation Tours 32
Chicago River Tours 42
Untouchable Tours 90

STAR ATTRACTIONS

CALENDAR OF EVENTS

Listed below is a selection of Chicagoland's most popular annual events. Please note that dates may change from year to year. For more detailed information, contact the Chicago Office of Tourism: 312-744-2400 or www.cityofchicago.org.

February

Chinese New Year Parade
Wentworth Ave. from
Cermak Rd. to 24th St.
312-744-3315
www.cityofchicago.org/
specialevents

March

Chicago Flower and Garden Show
Navy Pier
312-595-PIER
www.chicagoflower.com

St. Patrick's Day Parade
Columbus Dr., from Balbo Ave.
to Monroe St.
312-744-3315

April

Major League Baseball Opening Day

Chicago Cubs
Wrigley Field
773-404-2827
http://chicago.cubs.mlb.com

Chicago White Sox
U.S. Cellular Field
312-674-1000
www.chisox.com

May

ArtChicago
Merchandise Mart,
222 Merchandise Mart Plaza
800-677-6278
www.artchicago.com

Chicago Summer Neighborhood Festivals
Various locations (May–Sept)
312-744-3315
www.cityofchicago.org/
specialevents

International Antiques Fair
Merchandise Mart,
222 Merchandise Mart Plaza
800-677-6278
www.merchandisemart.com/
chicagoantiques

Mayor Daley's Kids and Kites Festival
Museum of Science and
Industry, 57th Street and
Lake Shore Drive
312-744-3315
www.cityofchicago.org/
specialevents

June

Chicago Blues Festival
Grant Park
312-744-3315
www.cityofchicago.org/
specialevents

Chicago Gospel Festival
Millennium Park
312-744-3315
www.chicagogospelmusic
festival.us

Old Town Art Fair
1763 N. Norh Park Ave.
312-337-1938
www.oldtownartfair.org

Ravinia Festival
Highland Park (Jun–Sept)
847-266-5100
www.ravinia.org

Taste of Chicago
Grant Park
312-744-3315
www.tasteofchicago.us

MUST KNOW

July
Grant Park Music Festival
  Grant Park
  312-742-7638
  www.grantparkmusic
  festival.com

August
Bud Billiken Day Parade
  King Dr. between 35th St. and
  55th St.
  312-536-3710
  www.budbillikenparade.com
Chicago Air & Water Show
  North Avenue Beach
  312-744-3315
  www.chicagoairand
  watershow.us
**Viva! Chicago Latin
Music Festival**
  Grant Park
  312-744-3315
  www.vivachicago.us

September
Celtic Fest Chicago
  Grant Park
  312-744-3315
  www.celticfestchicago.us
Chicago Jazz Festival
  Petrillo Bandshell, Grant Park
  312-744-3315
  www.chicagojazzfestival.us

World Music Festival
  Various locations
  312-742-1938
  www.cityofchicago.org/
  worldmusic

October
**Chicago International
Film Festival**
  Various theaters
  312-683-0121
  www.chicagofilmfestival.com
Chicago Marathon
  Ends at Grant Park
  312-904-9800
  www.chicagomarathon.com

November
Day of the Dead Celebration
  National Museum of Mexican
  Art, 1852 W. 19th St.
  312-738-1503
  www.nationalmuseumof
  mexicanart.org
Mag Mile Lights Festival
  N. Michigan Ave.
  312-642-3570
  www.themagnificentmile.com

December
Winter Wonder Fest
  Navy Pier (www.navypier.com)
  312-595-PIER

©Kenneth Ilio/Dreamstime.com

June: Taste of Chicago at Grant Park

CALENDAR OF EVENTS

11

PRACTICAL INFORMATION

WHEN TO GO

Spring is temperamental, with conditions fluctuating from cold to warm and back again.
Although open-air activities are limited, the winter and spring months can be a prime time to make the most of lower hotel rates and indoor treasures. **Summer** is the high tourist season, offering countless festivals and opportunities for outdoor recreation—along with hot and humid weather, and, often, rain (June, July and August are statistically the rainiest months). **Fall** is also popular, when crowds thin, the humidity disappears and the temperatures cool. Snow poses little threat until late November, when the infamous Chicago **winter** blows in: You'll be cold, but attractions won't be crowded.

KNOW BEFORE YOU GO

Before you go, consider obtaining maps and information about sightseeing, accommodations, travel packages, recreational opportunities and seasonal events.

Chicago Convention and Tourism Bureau
2301 S. Lakeshore Dr.,
Chicago, IL 60616
312-567-8500; www.choose chicago.com

Chicago Office of Tourism
78 E. Washington St.,
Chicago, IL 60602
312-744-2400; http://egov.cityof chicago.org

Visitor Information Centers
Chicago Cultural Center
78 E. Randolph St.; 312-744-6630
Open year-round Mon–Thu 8am–7pm, Fri 8am–6pm, Sat 10am–6pm, Sun 11am–5pm. Closed holidays.
Sears on State Information Kiosk
2 N. State St., at Madison Ave.
Open year-round Mon–Sat 10am–6pm, Sun noon–5pm. Closed Thanksgiving Day & Dec 25.

Average Seasonal Temperatures in Chicago				
	Jan	**Apr**	**July**	**Oct**
Avg. high	29°F/-2°C	58°F/15°C	83°F/28°C	63°F/18°C
Avg. low	13°F/-10°C	38°F/4°C	62°F/17°C	42°F/6°C

Useful Websites

Here are some additional Websites to help you plan your trip:

www.877chicago.com
www.themagnificentmile.com
www.chicagonews.com
www.choosechicago.com

www.metromix.com
www.chicago.il.org
www.chicagolandchamber.org

MUST KNOW

International Visitors

Visitors from outside the US can obtain information from the Chicago Convention and Tourism Bureau (*312-567-8500 or 877-244-2246; www.choosechicago.com*) or from the US embassy or consulate in their country of residence. For a complete list of American consulates and embassies abroad, visit the US State Department Bureau of Consular Affairs listing on the Internet at: *http://travel.state.gov*.

Entry Requirements

Travelers entering the United States under the Visa Waiver Program (VWP) must have a machine-readable passport. Any traveler without a machine-readable passport will be required to obtain a visa before entering the US. Citizens of VWP countries are permitted to enter the US for general business or tourist purposes for a maximum of 90 days without needing a visa. Requirements for the Visa Waiver Program can be found at the Department of State's Visa Services Web site (*http://travel.state.gov*). All citizens of nonparticipating countries must have a visitor's visa. Upon entry, nonresident foreign visitors must present a valid passport and round-trip transportation ticket. Canadian citizens are not required to present a passport or visa, but they must present a valid picture ID and proof of citizenship. Naturalized Canadian citizens should carry their citizenship papers.

US Customs

All articles brought into the US must be declared at the time of entry. Prohibited items include: plant material, firearms and ammunition (if not for sporting purposes), and meat or poultry products. For information, contact the US Customs Service, 1300 Pennsylvania Ave. NW, Washington, DC 20229 (*202-354-1000; www.cbp.gov*).

GETTING THERE

By Air

Chicago is serviced by two international airports:
O'Hare International Airport (ORD) is one of the world's busiest airports. Located 17 miles northwest of downtown, O'Hare is served by most major carriers *(take I-90 West to Exit 78/I-190 West; 773-686-2200 or 800-832-6352; www.ohare.com)*. **Midway International Airport (MDW)** has more commuter air traffic and is much less crowded than O'Hare. It's located 10 miles southwest of downtown *(take I-90 South to I-55 West to Exit 286/Cicero Ave.; 773-686-2200 or 800-832-6352; www.flychicago.com)*.
Airport Transfers – **Airport Express** offers shuttles between O'Hare, Midway, downtown hotels and North Shore suburbs year-round. Shuttles run between airports and downtown hotels daily. Agents available 6am–10:30pm; 24 hour reservations can be made online. *(888-284-3826; www.airportexpress.com; one passenger/one-way fare is $23 from O'Hare Airport)*. Tickets are available at Airport Express counters, located across from the baggage-claim areas.
Chicago Transit Authority trains service both airports: the Blue Line runs to the Loop from O'Hare; the Orange Line train services Midway *(for schedule and fare information, see p15)*.

Taxi service from the airports to downtown averages $30 to $35 from O'Hare and $25 to $30 from Midway.

By Train
Amtrak *(800-872-7245 or www. amtrak.com)* runs several lines to Chicago's Union Station, on the Near West Side *(210 S. Canal St.; 312-655-2524)*.

By Bus
Greyhound *(800-229-9424 or www.greyhound.com)* provides bus service to Chicago's main bus terminal, located on the Near West Side *(630 W. Harrison St.; 312-408-5800 or 800-231-2222)*. The new **Megabus** *(800-402-6342 or www. megabus.com)* has low-priced fares to other Midwestern cities. Bus stops vary according to the route.

By Car
Chicago is easily accessible from a number of major highways. The Dan Ryan Expressway (I-90/I-94), the Chicago Skyway (toll road) and I-57 serve the south side, while the Stevenson Expressway (I-55) offers access to the southwest. The Eisenhower Expressway (I-290), called Congress Parkway within downtown, provides the quickest route to the western suburbs. The Kennedy (I-90/94) and Edens (I-94) expressways serve the northwest and north sides respectively. Lake Shore Drive (US-41) follows the lakefront through the city to the northern suburbs. The I-294 (Tri-state Tollway) belt-way rings western Chicago.

GETTING AROUND

By Car
The interstates around Chicago tend to be heavily trafficked, no matter the time of day. Parking downtown can be a hassle; in general, you're better off walking or taking public transportation. If you do have a car, avoid driving during commuter rush hours *(weekdays 7:30am–9am & 4pm–6pm)*. Use of seat belts is required. Child safety seats are mandatory for children under 7 years of age.
Driving in the US – Visitors bearing valid driver's licenses issued by their country of residence are not required to obtain an International Driver's License. Drivers must carry vehicle registration and/or rental contract, and proof of automobile insurance at all times. Gasoline is sold by the gallon (1 gallon = 3.8 liters). Vehicles in the US are driven on the right-hand side of the road.
Parking – Street parking can be difficult to find and public parking garages are expensive (downtown garage parking averages $7 to $17 for one to four hours). Note that your vehicle will be towed from the street and some parking lots if left overnight.
Many streets are designated Snow Routes (indicated by red, white and blue signs); parking is not allowed on either side of these streets overnight during winter or when there are two or more inches of snow on the ground. No parking is allowed on many streets during rush hour and during specific street-cleaning days; check signs before you leave your car. Parking in some residential areas is restricted to area residents.

By Public Transportation

The **Chicago Transit Authority (CTA)** operates an efficient and extensive network of **subways**, elevated trains and trolleys. Schedules and route information are availbale at most train stations, as well as through the CTA *(888-968-7282 or www.transitchicago.com)*. **Pace Bus** *(847-364-7223; www.pacebus.com)* provides bus service throughout the suburbs. CTA route maps and brochures are available online, as well as at both airports, train stations, and at City of Chicago information booths. Chicago's **Travel Information Hotline** is available seven days a week *(4:45am–1am)* from any Chicago area code: *836-7000*.

Elevated Commuter Rail Line – *See map on inside back cover.* Known to locals as the "El," this elevated train runs through the Loop and connects all cardinal points of the city and suburbs through a system of colored lines such as the Red Line, running north–south; the Green Line, running west–south; the Blue Line, taking a west–northwest route through Wicker Park to O'Hare Airport; the Brown Line, a scenic,

Navy Pier Trolley

Want to take the kids to Navy Pier? Sure, you do! But it can be a hike from hotels in the Loop. Never fear. Hop aboard the free trolley that runs daily between the pier and State Street, along Grand Avenue and Illinois Street (trolley stops are marked with signs). Trolleys run about every 20 minutes *(Mon–Thu 10am–9pm, Fri & Sat 10am–11pm, Sun 10am–9pm).*

above-ground route running north; and the Orange Line, a connection to Midway Airport. Basic fare is $1.75; transfers are an extra 25¢ (for two transfers within two hours of ticket purchase). Trains operate daily 5am–1am; the Red and Blue lines operate 24 hours a day. **Visitor passes**, which allow unlimited rides on all CTA buses and trains, are available at train stations and visitor centers, or online *(1 day/$5; 2 days/$9; 3 days/$12; 5 days/$18)*. Purchase a fare card or visitor pass for access to city buses as well. Bus fares are $2 with exact cash, versus $1.75 with a fare card.

Chicago Greeters

First time in Chicago? Take a free tour with one of Chicago's official greeters *(312-744-8000; www.chicagogreeter.com; tours held Mon–Fri 9am–5pm)*. These savvy guides enjoy sharing their knowledge and love of the Windy City. Set aside a morning or afternoon to explore neighborhoods, parks, cultural elements, and, of course, the indispensable shops and restaurants. Tours can be one-on-one or group-oriented; "themed" tours offer jaunts for everyone from the literature buff to the sports enthusiast. Short on time? Try "Insta Greeter," the first-come, first-served free mini-tour; it lets you explore downtown in an hour with a local volunteer greeter. *www.chicagogreeter.com.*

Car Rental		
Car Rental Company	**Reservations**	**Internet**
Alamo	800-462-5266	www.alamo.com
Avis	800-331-1212	www.avis.com
Budget	800-527-0700	www.budget.com
Dollar	800-800-3665	www.dollar.com
Enterprise	800-261-7331	www.enterprise.com
Hertz	800-654-3131	www.hertz.com
National	800-227-7368	www.nationalcar.com
Thrifty	800-847-4389	www.thrifty.com

By Taxi

Cabs are readily available at all hours; you can hail cabs on the street, or find them outside major hotels. Riders are required to pay the fare shown on the meter, plus any tolls. The meter starts at $1.90 for the first mile, and $1.60 for each additional mile, or $2 for each minute of waiting time. Major cab companies include: **Flash Cab** *(773-561-4444; www.flashcab. com)*, **Yellow Cab** *(312-829-4222; www.yellowcabchicago.com)*, and **Checker Cab** *(312-243-2537)*.

By Water

From Memorial Day to Labor Day, **Shoreline Sightseeing** *(312-222-9328; www.shorelinesightseeing. com)* operates water taxis on Lake Michigan between Navy Pier and Shedd Aquarium, and along the Chicago River from Navy Pier to the Sears Tower. Fares for a one-way ticket are $6 for adults, and $3 for children under age 12. An all-day pas costs $12 for adults, $6 for children under 12.

By Foot

Put on your comfortable shoes. Walking is one of the best ways to explore Chicago, particularly The Loop, River North and the Magnificent Mile neighborhoods.

ACCESSIBILITY

Disabled Travelers

Federal law requires that businesses (including hotels and restaurants) provide access for the disabled, devices for the hearing impaired, and designated parking spaces. For further information, contact the Society for Accessible Travel and Hospitality **(SATH)** *(347 Fifth Ave., Suite 605, New York, NY 10016; 212-447-7284; www.sath.org)*. All national parks have facilities for the disabled, and offer free or discounted passes.

For details, contact the **National Park Service** *(Office of Public Inquiries, P.O. Box 37127, Room 1013, Washington, DC 20013-7127; 202-208-4747; www.nps.gov)*. Passengers who will need assistance with train or bus travel should give advance notice to Amtrak *(800-872-7245 or 800-523-*

6590/TDD; www.amtrak.com) or Greyhound (800-752-4841 or 800-345-3109/TDD; www.greyhound.com). Make reservations for hand-controlled cars in advance with the rental company.

Local Lowdown – Additional detailed information about access for the disabled in the Chicago area is available from the **Mayor's Office for People with Disabilities** (121 North LaSalle St.; Room 1104, Chicago, IL 60602; 312-744-7050; www.cityofchicago.org). They also publish a monthly newsletter called **AccessNotes**, which is available from their office. For information about disabled access to public transportation, contact the **Chicago Transit Authority** (312-432-7025; www.transitchicago.com).

Senior Citizens
Many hotels, attractions and restaurants offer discounts to visitors age 62 or older (proof of age may be required). The **AARP**, formerly the American Association of Retired Persons, offers discounts to its members (601 E St. NW, Washington, DC 20049; 202-424-3410; www.aarp.com).

ACCOMMODATIONS
For a list of suggested accommodations, see Must Stay.
An area visitors' guide including lodging directory is available free-of-charge from the Chicago Convention and Tourism Bureau (see p12).

Hotel Reservation Services
At Home Inn Chicago – 312-640-1050 or 800-375-7084. www.athomeinnchicago.com. Focuses on city-style B&B accommodations.

Hot Rooms – 773-468-7666 or 800-468-3500. www.hotrooms.com.
Hotel Reservations Network – 800-715-7666. www.hoteldiscount.com.
Hotels.com – 800-346-8357. www.hotels.com.
Illinois Hotel & Lodging Association – 877-456-3446. www.stayillinois.com.

Hostels
Hostels are a great choice for budget travelers. Prices average $17 to $35 per night for a dorm-style room.
Chicago International Hostel – 6318 N. Winthrop Ave., Lakeview. 773-262-1011. www.hostelworld.com.
Hostelling International Chicago – 24 E. Congress Pkwy. at Wabash St., in the Loop. 312-360-0300. www.hichicago.org.

COMMUNICATIONS

Area Codes
To call between different area codes in Chicago, dial 1 + area code + seven-digit number. The same applies to local calls, even within the same area code.

Chicago (downtown):	**312**
Chicago (other areas):	**773**
Northern suburbs (Evanston):	**847**
Southern suburbs (Oak Park):	**708**
Western suburbs:	**630**
Outer suburbs:	**815**

Internet Access
Free wireless internet access is available across Chicago; see www.wififreespot.com to find the nearest WiFi spot to you.
There are also plenty of internet cafés around the city; ask at visitor information centers or at your hotel.

PRACTICAL INFORMATION

Important Numbers	
Emergency (Police/Ambulance/Fire Department, 24hrs)	911
Police *(non-emergency, within Chicago)*	311
Poison Control	312-942-5969
Physician Referral	312-926-8400
Chicago Medical Society	312-670-2550
Dental Emergencies	
Chicago Dental Society	312-836-7300
24-hour Pharmacy: Walgreens	
757 N. Michigan Ave., Magnificent Mile	312-664-4000
111. S. Halsted St., Near West Side	312-463-9139
1601 N. Wells St., Old Town	312-642-4738
641 N. Clark St., South Loop	312-587-0904
Time	312-976-1616
Weather	312-976-1212

Newspapers

Chicago's two main daily morning newspapers are the *Chicago Tribune* and the *Chicago Sun-Times*. For news of what's going on when you're in town, check out the entertainment sections of the *Tribune* (Friday) and the *Sun Times* (*Weekend Plus* section), both published on Fridays.

Two weekly alternatives (published Thursday) are the *Chicago Reader* and *Time Out Chicago*. These offer good coverage of the arts and nightlife. A great resource for last-minute dining and nightlife events is *http://312diningdiva.com*.

DISCOUNTS

To find Chicago's many discounted offers, start with a look at *www.chicagoofficeoftourism.org/specialValues*.

Some of the main discounted passes to benefit from are:

CityPass – *$59 adults; $49 children ages 4–11; good for nine consecutive days*. This gives you discounted admission to some of the major attractions. You can purchase a CityPass at participating attractions, or at *www.citypass.com*.

Metra 10-Ticket Ride – 15% off one-way fares on city rail. *http://metrarail.com*.

$5 Weekend Pass – Unlimited city rail travel at the weekend (not South Shore).

GoChicago Card – *Available for 1, 3, 5, or 7 days, from $59 to $135 adults; $44.99 to $110.49 children*. An all-access pass to all kinds of attractions, and a free guided tour per day. *www.gochicagocard.com*

ELECTRICITY

Voltage in the US is 120 volts AC, 60 Hz. Foreign-made appliances may need AC adapters (available at specialty travel and electronics stores) and North American flat-blade plugs.

MONEY AND CURRENCY EXCHANGE

Visitors can exchange currency downtown in the Loop at the **Northern Trust Company** *(50 S. LaSalle St.; 312-630-6000; www. northerntrust.com; open Mon–Fri 9am–5pm)*, **World's Money Exchange, Inc.** *(203 N. LaSalle St., Suite M-11; 312-641-2151; www. wmeinc.com; open Mon–Fri 9am–5pm)*, and **American Express Travel Service** *(605 N. Michigan Ave.; 312-943-7840; or 55 West Monroe St.; 312-541-5440 www. americanexpress.com; open Mon–Fri 8:30am–5:30pm)*. **American Express®** also has an office on the Magnificent Mile *(605 N. Michigan Ave., Suite 105; 312-435-2570; open Mon–Fri 8:30am–6pm, Sat 9am–5pm)*. **O'Hare International Airport Currency Exchange** offices *(773 686-7965)* are located on the lower level of the international terminal, at Arrivals Door A. For cash transfers, **Western Union** *(800-325-6000; www.westernunion. com)* has agents throughout Chicago. Banks, stores, restaurants and hotels accept traveler's checks with photo identification.

To report a lost or stolen credit card: **American Express®** *(800-528-4800)*; **Diners Club®** *(800-234-6377)*; **MasterCard®** *(800-307-7309)*; **Visa®** *(800-336-8472)*.

OPENING HOURS

Visiting Attractions
Most attractions open their doors at 9am and close them at 5pm. Be sure to check before visiting.

Shopping
Stores tend to open Mon–Sat 10am–6 or 7pm, Sun noon–6pm.

SMOKING
Despite a number of opposers, Chicago followed other cities around the world by imposing a smoking ban in 2008. Public places, including restaurants, clubs and theaters are all smoke free.

SPECTATOR SPORTS
Sports are as essential a part of Chicago as the wind, the lake and deep-dish pizza. If you are at all inclined, watching a sport should be on your "to do" list. Availability of tickets is in direct proportion to how well the team in question is doing. If the Bears are Super Bowl-bound, you won't find a ticket at all, and even when they aren't, **American football** tickets can be expensive bought from a ticket broker. **Basketball** (the Bulls) and **baseball** (the Cubs and the White Sox) are generally available during the regular season. Since Americans haven't embraced hockey and soccer as they have other sports, Blackhawks and Fire tickets are easy to find. No matter what team you see, you're sure to encounter enthusiastic fans and a quintessential Chicago experience.

TAXES AND TIPPING
Prices displayed in Chicago do not include sales tax of 10.25%, which is not reimbursable. It is customary to give a gift of money—a tip— for services rendered, to waiters (15–20% of bill), porters ($1 per bag), chamber maids ($1 per day) and cab drivers (15% of fare).

TIME ZONE
Chicago is in the **Central Time** (CT) zone, one hour behind New York City and six hours behind Greenwich Mean Time.

PRACTICAL INFORMATION

CHICAGO, ILLINOIS

Chicago (population close to 3 million) was never destined to be a great city; the odds, from the get-go, were stacked against it. But mud, fire, labor unrest, gangsters, shady politics and the Cubs only seem to have strengthened Chicago's character. Settled in 1779 by Jean-Baptiste Point du Sable on a swampy riverbank, Chicago takes its name from the native Potawatomi word She-caw-gu, meaning "stinking onion"—a reference to the garlic that grew wild in the area.

Chicago Grows Up – At first glance, it is hard to understand how and why Chicago turned from a mere town of 4,000 in 1837, when the city was incorporated, to 300,000 people by 1871 and 1.5 million at the turn of the 20C. The quagmire on which the city was built thwarted construction and contributed to the spread of disease. In the 1850s, Chicago stank. Much-needed sewer lines were placed at street level and

the streets and structures raised around them. To stem overflow and sewage dumped into the Chicago River, and to protect drinking water and prevent cholera, a scheme was hatched to reverse the river's flow away from the lake. By 1900 engineers finally succeeded in permanently reversing the river's flow.

Despite those setbacks, Chicago's location between the Mississippi River and the Great Lakes became a strategic advantage for a growing America. Lumber, grain and livestock funneled through Chicago in extraordinary quantities. Tunnels, bridges and roads were built to accommodate the busy metropolis, and immigrants arrived in droves to do the work. In October 1871, the **Great Chicago Fire** broke out, burning

Carl Sandburg's Chicago

"Hog Butcher for the World,
Tool Maker, Stacker of Wheat,
Player with Railroads and the
Nation's Freight Handler:
Stormy, husky, brawling,
City of the Big Shoulders . . ."

Carl Sandburg, 1916, *"Chicago"*

Engraving of The Burning of Chicago (c. 1883) by R. H. Stoddard

Photo: ©Constance McGuire/iStockphoto.com

INTRODUCTION

Navy Pier with Chicago skyline

for three days and destroying the central city. Stubborn and proud locals began rebuilding immediately and growth continued unabated; the population tripled in the decade following the fire. In spite of crowding, poor sanitation and grueling working conditions, Chicago rose above the murk of its stockyards and steel mills. After 1880, the central city grew tall on the talents of a coterie of architects who pioneered the Chicago School of Architecture.

By the 1890s, elite residents had leisure time and money enough to establish cultural institutions. The crowning achievement would be the staging of the **World's Columbian Exposition** *(see p67)* in 1893 on the South Side lakefront. A showcase of Neoclassical architecture and modern technology, the fair established Chicago as a world-class city.

Bootleggers and Power Brokers – The Roaring Twenties left a permanent mark, as bootlegging gangsters, the best-known being **Al Capone**, murdered many in attempts to control the illegal liquor business. Another power broker came into its own when the

Democratic Machine hit its stride under Richard J. Daley in 1955. His "City that Works" did so because the mayor knew how to exchange influence to get things done. Daley died in 1976. When Harold Washington, the city's first black mayor, triumphantly took office in 1983, many looked forward to a new chapter. However, Washington died unexpectedly in office four years later. Waiting in the wings, Richard M. Daley rose to assume the throne. He has emerged as his father's son, for better and worse, and the city's complicated history continues in the 21C.

Chicago Fast Facts and Firsts

- Chicago covers 228 square miles.
- The city is home to 2.8 million people.
- Chicago invented the zipper, Twinkies, and the smoke-filled room.
- Chicago birthed the first skyscraper and the first controlled atomic reaction.
- In 2007 alone, 91 movies and TV shows were filmed in Chicago.
- The Chicago Board of Trade is the world's oldest and largest futures exchange.

CITY OF BIG SHOULDERS

NEIGHBORHOODS

Chicago is a city of neighborhoods—urban, busy, sometimes crowded, yes, but also tree-lined and intimate. From the Far South Side, up through Bronzeville and Chinatown, around Pilsen, and then through the Loop into the upscale neighborhoods of the Magnificent Mile and the Gold Coast, to the North Side's vibrancy, the patchwork that is Chicago offers something new, literally, around each corner.

THE LOOP★★★

See map on inside front cover.

Looming large along the lakefront, south of the Chicago River, the city's busy Loop has been fertile ground for architectural innovation since the fire in 1871 destroyed the downtown business district. Named for the elevated tracks that circle them, these blocks bustle with workday energy as Chicagoans transact their daily business in office towers that catalog the city's skyward growth since the 19th century. **State Street★** has renewed its traditional role as a busy shopping corridor *(see pp26, 103)*, and in the evenings, the Loop offers a selection of theater, music and dining experiences.

In the Loop

Auditorium Building★★★

50 E. Congress Pkwy. 312-431-2360. www.auditoriumtheatre.org. Theater may be visited by guided tour only; reservations required; call ahead for times.

This solid cornerstone of the Loop's east side launched the careers of renowned architects Louis Sullivan and Dankmar Adler,

Auditorium Building

©Chicago Architecture Foundation/Anne Evans

as well as a young draftsman named Frank Lloyd Wright *(see p79).*

Looping the Loop

Most Chicagoans agree that the best way to explore the Loop is on foot. However, the city offers some fun alternative methods of getting around this neighborhood:

By Boat – The best way to see Chicago's skyscrapers is from the river. Cruises depart from the docks on both sides of the Michigan Avenue Bridge, near the **Riverwalk★**, a great place for a stroll in nice weather.

For more information on river tours, see p42.

By the "L" – Take the elevated Brown Line (Ravenswood) to circle the Loop.

By Train – A free 40-minute train tour affords the same views as the "L" *(offered on a first-come, first-served basis May–Sept, Sat 11:35am & 12:55pm).*

Public Sculpture in the Loop

Chicago Stock Exchange Arch
· Dankmar Adler and Louis Sullivan
Art Institute, Columbus Dr. entrance
Monument with Standing Beast
· Jean Dubuffet
James R. Thompson Center Plaza
The Seated Lincoln
· Augustus Saint-Gaudens
Grant Park, Court of Presidents
Untitled
· Pablo Picasso *Daley Center Plaza*

Flamingo
· Alexander Calder
Federal Center Plaza
Four Seasons
· Marc Chagall
First National Bank Plaza

Miró's Chicago
· Joan Miró
*Washington St., next to
Chicago Temple*

Completed in 1889, it housed a hotel, an office tower and a theater and was Chicago's tallest building at the time. The spectacular theater remains an acoustic marvel; enter the lobby on Congress Parkway to see some of Sullivan's intricate designs. Better yet, reserve tickets for one of the dance or musical theater productions held here between November and June.

Former Location of Carson Pirie Scott & Company★★★

1 S. State St.

Architect Louis Sullivan's incredible skill with ornament is evident in the cast iron that embroiders the building's rounded front corner. Indeed, this 1899 structure represents the height of Sullivan's ornamental genius. It was once one of State Street's duo of historic department stores. Development is underway to convert the space into a gourmet grocery, restaurant and retail and office space.

Chicago Cultural Center★★

78 E. Washington St. 312-744-6630. http://egov.cityofchicago.org. Open year-round Mon–Thu 8am–7pm, Fri 8am–6pm, Sat 9am–6pm, Sun 10am–6pm. Closed major holidays.

This marvelous Neoclassical palace served as the city's first library when it was completed in 1897. Today it functions as an all-purpose exhibition, arts and music center, and also houses the **Chicago Office of Tourism Visitor Information Center** *(312-744-2400).*
Enter from Washington Street and ascend the grand staircase to **Preston-Bradley Hall★** (note the Tiffany stained-glass dome), where free concerts are offered Monday through Friday at 12:15pm and on Sunday at 3pm.

Former Carson Pirie Scott & Company Building

©Chicago Architecture Foundation/Anne Evans

Chicago Cultural Center

City of Chicago/Hedrich Blessing

Chicago School of Architecture

Fortunately, without a time machine you can get a glimpse of what 19th century Chicago looked like while you're in the Loop.
For a sense of scale, head to the 16-story **Monadnock Building★★** *(53 W. Jackson Blvd.)*, the tallest masonry structure in Chicago; the **Marquette Building★★** *(140 S. Dearborn St.)*, whose lobby features a stunning **Tiffany glass mosaic** illustrating the journeys of French explorer Jacques Marquette; and

---

Touring Tip

For a good panorama of the north side of the river, venture to the corner of Clark Street and Wacker Drive. That massive pile to the left is the **Merchandise Mart**, all 4.1 million square feet of it *(see box, p106)*. To the right, the corncob towers of Marina City stand out, and just east of them, the IBM Building. Below it, the *Sun-Times* headquarters and printing press once stood; it was demolished in 2004 to make way for the new Trump Tower, scheduled for completion in 2009.

---

the **Rookery★★** *(southeast corner of LaSalle & Adams Sts.)*, which some think was named for the pigeons who invaded a temporary city hall erected here in 1871. Once your eye becomes familiar with the style, you'll spot many others.

Federal Center★★

On Dearborn St., between Adams St. & Jackson Blvd.

Completed in 1974, this three-building complex is a wonderful example of the steel-and-glass International style for which architect Ludwig Mies van der Rohe became so famous.
Though unadorned, its beauty depends on its perfect proportions. The restrained buildings form a perfect frame for Alexander Calder's fiery, flamboyant sculpture **Flamingo** (1973).

James R. Thompson Center★★

100 Randall St. Bounded by Clark, LaSalle, Randolph & Lake Sts.

Architectural "bad boy" Helmut Jahn, known for bucking accepted trends, designed this State of Illinois facility to resemble the domes you're used to seeing on government buildings. Though quirky, the shape makes possible the soaring **atrium**, which rises the full 17 stories and encloses open office floors. Catch a snack at the lower-level food court and enjoy the constantly changing play of light and shadow that filters into the airy space. **Monument with Standing Beast**, a curvaceous fiberglass sculpture by Jean Dubuffet, adorns the plaza.

Scraping the Sky

A talented and energetic group of architects—William Le Baron Jenney, Louis Sullivan, William Holabird, Martin Roche, Daniel Burnham, John Wellborn Root and others—rebuilt Chicago after the 1871 fire. Within a year, 10,000 new buildings rose up at a cost of $45 million. By 1890 the booming population needed more offices. With no place to go but up, Chicago architects and engineers created the skyscraper. In traditional masonry construction, thick walls support the weight of the building, but architect William Le Baron Jenney (1832–1907) reversed the formula by hanging "curtain" walls on a skeletal steel frame, allowing buildings to grow taller. Based on this steel-frame construction, Jenney's 1884 now demolished, nine-story Home Insurance Building is considered the first modern skyscraper. Engineers mastered ways to anchor tall buildings in Chicago's swampy soil and to reduce the effects of high winds. Improvements to the elevator and the telephone made vertical height practical.

Thus, the **Chicago School of Architecture** was born, recognized as the first significant new movement in architecture since the Italian High Renaissance.

Richard J. Daley Center★★

Bounded by Washington, Clark, Randolph & Dearborn Sts.

The Daley Center is probably best known for its plaza, where Picasso's fantastic steel creature holds court. Chicagoans shuddered at first, but the beast may now be as famous (and beloved) as "Hizzoner da Mare" himself, who governed the city from 1955 to 1976. Housing courtrooms and offices, this fine example of the International style of architecture was completed in 1965 (at the time, it was the city's tallest building). Seasonal festivities, topical rallies, protests and a summertime farmers' market take place under the Picasso.

Chicago Board of Trade Building★

141 W. Jackson Blvd. 312-435-7180. www.cbotbuilding.com.

Hog futures, anyone? The Board of Trade was founded in 1848 to regulate trade of the Midwest's

Richard J. Daley Center

City of Chicago

bountiful agricultural commodities. This outstanding Art Deco skyscraper (1930, Holabird & Root) testifies to that abundance, anchoring the south end of the LaSalle Street financial district. Ceres, the goddess of the harvest, gazes down from high atop the building's soaring roof. Today all the action takes place inside on the 60,000-square-foot trading floors, where frenetic traders in brightly colored jackets buy and sell stock options and commodities. But, even if you don't go inside, you can get a sense of the building's heft and significance by looking at how it anchors the canyon of skyscrapers on LaSalle Street.

Macy's State St. ★

111 N. State St. 312-781-1000. www.macys.com. Open year-round Mon–Fri 10am–8pm, Sat 9am–10pm, Sun 11am–6pm. Closed major holidays.

This grand old department store occupies an entire block at the north end of fabled State Street. It was completed in stages between 1892 and 1914 by D.H. Burnham & Co., and its richly embellished corner clock remains a Chicago icon, despite the fact that its name changed from Marshall Field's

Macy's on State Street with the landmark clock

to Macy's in 2006. The interior features over a million square feet of retail space and a lovely Tiffany favrile dome. If you're in town around the holidays, take in the legendary decorated windows and have lunch under the 45-foot Christmas tree in the Walnut Room restaurant, both traditions that Macy's kept intact when it took over Field's.

State Street ★

The song that made State Street—"that great street"—famous ("Chicago" by Fred Fisher) dates back to 1922, when merchants liked to call the intersection at State and Madison streets the "World's Busiest Corner." True or not, *everybody* crowded State Street in those days: shoppers, movie and theatergoers,

Meals at Macy's

Macy's is a great place to go when you get hungry; the department store has a restaurant for every taste. On the 7th floor, the white-tablecloth **Walnut Room** *(312-781-3125)* conjures up bygone days when genteel gloved and hatted ladies lunched in the middle of their busy shopping day. You'll find a lighter lunch and soda-fountain desserts at the **Frango Café** *(312-781-2945)*, where you can also buy Chicago's Frango mints, though Field's famous candies are no longer made here. **Seven on State** *(312-781-3693)* serves grilled Thai shrimp, ham crêpes and other upscale dishes in a sleek food-court setting. For burgers and pub fare, try **Infield's** *(800-634-3537)*, where nonshoppers can catch up on their sports news.

MUST SEE

office workers. But State Street had been great since the 1860s when real-estate magnate Potter Palmer bought a stretch of the muddy, narrow byway. He convinced the city council to widen it, replaced rundown shacks with the elegant Palmer House Hotel, and lured Field, Leiter and Company from Lake Street by building them a new department store. Suddenly, State Street was *the* place to be. Though all was destroyed by the 1871 fire, the street came back with a vengeance. As you stroll the blocks between Wacker and Congress, look for signs recounting more State Street history *(www. chicagoloopalliance.com)*. Don't skip the 19th century glamour of the 1895 **Reliance Building★★** *(32 N. State St.)*, now reincarnated as the **Hotel Burnham** *(see p148)*. Its renovation makes it one of the few architectural treasures you can still see and appreciate from both the exterior and the interior.

MAGNIFICENT MILE★★★

The Champs Elysées of Chicago, this promenade along **North Michigan Avenue**, from the Chicago River north to Oak Street, is the city's most prestigious thoroughfare, blooming with plantings in the summer and twinkling with holiday lights all winter. Lined with exclusive boutiques and large retail stores, luxury hotels and premier residential and office high rises, the "Boul Mich" has come a long way from its beginnings as an ordinary city street. Its most distinctive relics survived the Great Fire in 1871; the bizarre 1869 **Water Tower★** *(see p42)* still stands toward the north end at Chicago Avenue. The opening of the **Michigan Avenue Bridge★** *(Wacker Dr. & N. Michigan Ave.)* joined the north and south sides of the city in 1920, igniting an incredible building boom that spawned most of the original landmarks on the avenue. The **John Hancock Center★★★** *(see p38)* and **Water Tower Place★** *(no. 835)* ushered in a new era of skyscrapers and retailing in the early 1970s when Michigan Avenue displaced **State Street★** as the city's shopping corridor *(see pp26, 103)*.

Along the Boulevard

Sights below are arranged in geographical order, from south to north. See map, p28–29.

Wrigley Building★★

400-410 N. Michigan Ave.

Set majestically on the north side of the river, this sparkling structure was built in two stages (30 stories to the south in 1920 and 21 to the north in 1924, both designed

©Chicago Architecture Foundation/Anne Evans

Wrigley Building

by Graham, Anderson, Probst & White). The white terra-cotta exterior, its six subtle shades chosen to add more luster at the top, is particularly stunning when it's lit up at night.

Tribune Tower★★

435 N. Michigan Ave.

Corporate headquarters of the Tribune Company's vast empire, this soaring tower (Hood & Howells), built in 1925, is a true "cathedral of commerce." Besides its dramatic Gothic style, the "Trib Tower" is known for the fragments and stones from the world's famous structures and sites that were collected by *Tribune* correspondents and embedded in its exterior walls. Look closely to find stones from the Berlin Wall, Omaha Beach, the Taj Mahal, and 117 others.

InterContinental Chicago★

505 N. Michigan Ave.
312-944-4100.
www.interconti.com.
See p141.

The gold-leaf dome atop this 41-story building was a popular design among the Shriners, a Masonic fraternity, for whom the building was constructed as an athletic club in 1929. Step through its heavy bronze doors into a quasi-Eastern fantasia of design. Today's modern hotel (opened in 1990) retains the club's opulent Oriental decoration.
If you can, head up to the 14th floor to see Olympic-size swimming pool, nestled under an opulently-decorated ceiling.

MAGNIFICENT MILE

Hotels
- Allerton Crowne Plaza
- Chicago's Lenox Suites Hotel
- The Drake Hotel
- Fitzpatrick Chicago
- Four Seasons
- InterContinental Chicago
- Le Meridien
- Millennium Knickerbocker Hotel
- The Peninsula Chicago
- The Raphael
- Red Roof Inn
- Seneca Hotel
- Sofitel Chicago Water Tower
- Talbott Hotel
- The Tremont Hotel
- W Chicago Lakeshore
- The Whitehall Hotel

Fourth Presbyterian Church★

N. Michigan Ave. at Delaware Pl.
312-787-4570. www.fourthchurch.
org. Open year-round daily
9am–5pm. Closed major holidays.

John Hancock Center
★★★ JOHN HANCOCK CENTER
900 N. Michigan Shops
★ Drake Hotel
One Magnificent Mile
★ Oak Street
Oak Street Beach
★ Fourth Presbyterian
H&M
Filene's Basement
Water Tower
Park Tower
Loyola University Water Tower Campus
American Girl Place
Looksglass Theatre
Hot Tix
★ Water Tower Place
★ Pumping Station
Seneca Park
★★ 860-880
Mies van der Rohe
Olympia Centre
Chicago Place
★★★ MAGNIFICENT
Neiman Marcus
Allerton Crowne Plaza
Niketown Chicago
★ Museum of Contemporary Art
Chicago
Lake Shore Park
Northwestern University Chicago Campus
VA-Lakeside Hospital
Lake Shore Place
★ STREETERVILLE
LAKE MICHIGAN
Ohio Street Beach
Jane Addams Park
River East Plaza
CENTER

0   1/10 mi
0   200 m

Restaurants
1 Bistro 110
2 Heaven on Seven
● The Saloon
3 Spiaggia
4 Tru
5 Wow Bao

Duck into this quiet sanctuary to escape Michigan Avenue's hustle and bustle. Dedicated in 1914, the church is an elegant reminder of Michigan Avenue's bygone character. A blend of French and English Gothic styles, the church seats 1,500 people and is softly lit by stunning medieval-style stained-glass windows. Controversy swirls today around the high-rise condominiums planned for the airspace above this lovely place of worship.

The Magnificent Mile Lights Festival

Chicagoans love festivals and fireworks, and not just in the summer. Michigan Avenue dresses up for the holidays on the weekend before Thanksgiving with the Magnificent Mile Lights Festival. A Saturday of music, ice carving and performances up and down the avenue culminates with the illumination of more than a million twinkling lights and a parade led by Mickey Mouse. Fireworks over the Chicago River end the evening with a bang. Stores are open late if you want to get a jump on your holiday shopping. *www.themagnificentmile.com.*

©Magnificent Mile®

Oak Street★

Between N. Michigan Ave. & Rush St. See p103.

One of the city's swankiest streets, Oak Street is worthy of a stroll, even if you don't intend to shop. As you would on Rodeo Drive or Madison Avenue, you may want to dress the part before hitting the sidewalk. Restaurants and bars balance out the boutiques for non-shoppers.

The Drake Hotel★

140 E. Walton St. 312-787-2200. www.thedrakehotel.com. See p140.

Grand dame of Chicago's luxury hotels, the Drake retains its 1920s atmosphere. At the top of

Michigan Avenue, it overlooks Oak Street Beach and Lake Shore Drive. Admire the plush red-velvet wall coverings, the wooden caisson ceiling and the elegant **Palm Court** in the dignified lobby. No visit to the Drake is complete without **English-style high tea** *(daily 1pm–5pm; reservations recommended).* Sip Darjeeling tea amid lush plantings and silken furniture, nibbling on tiny sandwiches, scones and clotted cream.

Museum of Contemporary Art★
See p54. 220 E. Chicago Ave.

American Girl Place
See p100. 111 E. Chicago Ave.

Streeterville★

Between the lake and North Michigan Avenue, **Streeterville** was settled in the 1880s by Capt. George Streeter, who declared it the "District of Lake Michigan," separate from the city of Chicago. Bounded on the south by the Chicago River, the area is the home of Northwestern University's Chicago campus and the residential towers at **860-880 North Lake Shore Drive★★**, which established the high-rise influence of modern architect Ludwig Mies van der Rohe in the early 1950s. To the east lies **Navy Pier★★** *(see pp15, 87, 97).*

RIVER NORTH★★

Between the Chicago River & North Branch, and Oak St. & Michigan Ave. www.rivernorthassociation.com.

Bounded on the west and south by the Chicago River, this neighborhood includes Wolf Point at the river's bend, one of Chicago oldest areas of settlement. Early industries and shantytowns established themselves along the river, while the northeast corner sprouted mansions and cathedrals. Over the decades, working class, immigrant, bohemian and wealthy residents staked claims around this neighborhood, which now claims many of the city's best galleries, restaurants and nightclubs.

Newberry Library★★

60 W. Walton St. 312-943-9090. www.newberry.org. Reading rooms open year-round Tue–Thu 10am–6pm, Fri–Sat 9am–5pm. Closed major holidays.

Want to look up your family tree? This respected institution, completed in 1893, ranks among the top independent research libraries in the country for genealogists and scholars in the humanities. Rotating exhibits—on such diverse topics as *Alice in Wonderland* and *King Arthur*—draw heavily on the library's collections and offer the general public an opportunity to sample the rare book, manuscript and map treasures. A look around the lobby will give you a good sense of the building's grandeur.

Marina City★

300 N. State St.

From the river's edge rise the twin "corncob" towers of Bertrand Goldberg's experimental urban community. Revolutionary when conceived in 1959, the complex, which includes apartments as well as entertainment and services, was an attempt to encourage young professionals to settle in the city.

Gallery Hopping in River North
The **River North Gallery District** *(see p107)* spans an eight-square-block area in River North. You'll find dozens of galleries here exhibiting an array of styles and media. On certain Friday evenings each month *(5pm–8pm)*, the galleries open their new shows *(for schedules, check online at www.chicago gallerynews.com or pick up a free copy of Chicago Gallery News).*

The Marina Towers' cast-concrete construction and rippling surfaces contrast dramatically with the "glass boxes" so popular at the time.

Merchandise Mart

See p106. 300 N. Wells St.

Marina City at night

©PhotoDisc

GOLD COAST★

Between Oak St. & North Ave., and extending west from the lake to LaSalle St.

This slice of Chicago's lakefront has been home to the city's well-to-do for more than a century. While all but a few of the mansions that once lined Lake Shore Drive have been demolished, you can still step back a century with a walk along State Parkway and landmark **Astor Street★★**, where quaint Victorian town houses and graystones occupy tiny, beautifully cultivated lots.

Chicago Architecture Foundation Tours

Throughout the year, knowledgeable docents at the Chicago Architecture Foundation (CAF) lead 78 different neighborhood walks. And lest you feel timid about architecture, fear not. These excellent tours make stone and steel come alive, and you'll meet some of Chicago's most interesting characters along the way.
For schedules and fees, contact CAF headquarters at the **ArchiCenter**
(224 S. Michigan Ave.; 312-922-3432, ext. 240; www.architecture.org).

Charnley-Persky House★

*1365 Astor St., at Schiller St.
312-915-0105. www.sah.org;
www.charnleyhouse.org.
Visit by one-hour guided tour only
year-round Wed at noon (free).
Sat tours offered Apr–Nov 10am
& 1pm, Dec–Mar 10am ($5).*

With its plain brick and limestone façade and horizontal form, the Charnley-Persky House stands out amid the Victorian residential architecture that was popular at the turn of the century.
Architect Louis Sullivan (with some input by his draftsman Frank Lloyd Wright) designed the house in 1892 for lumberman James Charnley. Inside, 11 rooms surround a central atrium; the kitchen is located in the narrow basement.

Oak Street Beach
*See p91.
Lake Shore Dr. at Oak St.*

Atrium, Charnley-Persky House

Charnley-Persky House/Donald G.Kalec

ANDERSONVILLE

Bounded by Winnemac & Elmdale Aves., and Ravenswood & Magnolia Aves.

In the 19th century, Swedish immigrant farmers were drawn to this outlying community because it was one of the few areas where poorer landowners could build wood, instead of more expensive brick or stone, homes. Now a central fixture of the city's North Side, Andersonville kept its Swedish roots, but is also home to a thriving gay and lesbian population, and an eclectic mix of other city-dwellers. Andersonville is dotted with great restaurants (Swedish and otherwise), home-décor boutiques and dance and nightclubs.

Clark Street
See p104.

Swedish-American Museum Center
See p104. 5211 N. Clark St.

LITTLE SAIGON

Argyle Ave. between Broadway & Sheridan Rd.

Just southeast of Andersonville, by a matter of blocks, is the tiny heart of the city's Vietnamese community. You'll know you've arrived when you see the uniquely-topped Asian-style El station that spans Argyle Avenue. (If you can, take the El here and exit at this stop. Parking in the neighborhood can be a challenge.)
Some locals refer to this area as "New Chinatown," because of its multi-Asian influences and to distinguish it from the South Side's Chinatown *(see p36)*. While it is small, this community is active and crowded day and night. Come here hungry, as every block is packed with small Pho shops and other authentic Vietnamese restaurants and grocery stores. You'll also find solid Thai, Japanese and Chinese eateries, including some dim sum brunches on the weekends.

LINCOLN SQUARE

Northwest of downtown. Lincoln Ave, bounded by Montrose and Lawrence Aves.

As Andersonville was the historic neighborhood for Swedish immigrants, Lincoln Square (not to be confused with Lincoln Park, *see p65*) was home to the city's many German settlers. The highlight of Lincoln Square is the brick-lined, pedestrian-friendly stretch of Lincoln Ave., between Leland and Lawrence Aves. Here you'll find pastry shops, bookstores, toy stores and outdoor plazas with live music (when weather permits). Many high-end Lakeview bars and restaurants have migrated to Lincoln Square in recent years, making the neighborhood a hot spot for nightlife, either before or after a concert at the **Old Town School of Folk Music** *(4544 N. Lincoln Ave.; 773-728-6000; www.oldtownschool.org).*

Sulzer Regional Library
4455 N. Lincoln Ave.

More than a mere branch of the public library, Sulzer (named after one of the neighborhood's first residents) is a destination for those who want to research Chicago's history, thanks to a unique collection of source materials. Furnishings were custom-designed to reflect the neighborhood's German roots.

Old Town School of Folk Music
544 N. Lincoln Ave.

OLD TOWN★

Bounded by Division, Halsted & LaSalle Sts., and Armitage Ave.

Working-class German families settled this area in the 1840s and 50s, and by 1900, North Avenue—the German Broadway—was alive with shops, bakeries, taverns and delicatessens. In the early 20th century, as the Germans moved north, the neighborhood fell into disrepair. It remained largely so until the low rents began to attract an artistic clientele in the mid-19th century. In 1959 **The Second City** comedy improv theater *(see p118)* took root here. The area's funky reputation lingered into the 1990s, now having all but disappeared as the 21st century ushered in a retail and residential building boom in Old Town and environs. Take a walk through Old Town Triangle (bounded roughly by North & Lincoln Aves.) to get a sense of the way people lived in the 1800s.

Menomonee Street★
The 300 block of this quaint street is the essence of Old Town. Nine cottages, **nos. 325–345**, are good examples of the small wooden cottages originally built here; they could be erected in no time using "balloon framing." This building innovation was accountable for the rapid growth and combustibility of the city. The tiny house at no. 216 is a rare example of a fire-relief shanty, a one-room dwellings built with funds donated by the Chicago Fire Relief and Aid Society for families left homeless by the fire.

Old Town Art Fair
A neighborhood fund-raising initiative begun in 1947 evolved into the Old Town Art Fair, which today draws thousands of art lovers to the area just north of North Avenue the second weekend in June. The premier fair features more than 250 artists, a silent jewelry auction, food, music and more *($5 donation requested).*
For more information, contact the Old Town Triangle Association: 312-337-1938 or www.oldtownartfair.org.

Chicago History Museum★
See p54. 1600 North Ave.

PILSEN

Southwest of downtown, from the Chicago River west to the city limits.

Pilsen started out in the 19th century as the largest settlement of Bohemian immigrants in the country. Over the years, Germans, Irish, Polish and Lithuanians passed through here, and today Pilsen forms the core of Chicago's enormous Hispanic population. The neighborhood, which centers on Halsted and 18th streets, also attracts artists, who open their studios in late September or early October each year for the **Pilsen East Artists Open House** *(312-738-8000)*. You can see much of Pilsen's art, however—in the form of large, colorful murals—on any excursion down 18th Street. Taquerias, markets and shops line the street as well; stop by **Restaurante Nuevo Leon** *(1515 W. 18th St.; 312-421-1517)* for a delicious traditional Mexican meal served in a family atmosphere. In late July, the **Fiesta del Sol** livens up the blocks from Throop to Morgan streets with outdoor music, food and fun *(312-666-2663; www.fiestadelsol.org)*.

National Museum of Mexican Art
1852 W. 19th St. See p58.

BUCKTOWN AND WICKER PARK

Northwest of downtown, from the Chicago River west to Western Ave., and Webster Ave. & Division St.

What SoHo was to Manhattan, Bucktown and Wicker Park were to Chicago. These adjacent neighborhoods (often lumped together as one) attracted creatively-rich but cash-poor designers and artists in the late 1980s and early 90s, thanks to big, open loft spaces with low rents. As was the case in SoHo, artists soon got priced out of their affordable neighborhood, but the artsy vibe remains. This is one of the city's best areas for boutique shopping, happening nightlife, interesting restaurants and excellent people-watching.

Flat Iron Arts Building

1579 N. Milwaukee Ave.

The 1913 Greek Revival building that occupies the triangle at the corner of Damen, Milwaukee and Aves. is the geographic and emotional heart of these neighborhoods. Originally designed by architects Holabird & Roche, today it is home to more than 30 artists' studios. It is also ground zero for Around the Coyote, the neighborhood's twice-annual art crawl-cum-street festival.

Damen and Milwaukee Avenues
See p105.

BRIDGEPORT, BRONZEVILLE AND CHINATOWN

South of downtown, both sides of the I 90-94 Expressway, south to 35th St.

This is trio is a melting pot of South Side neighborhoods. Bridgeport was traditionally the neighborhood in which Irish immigrants settled. But today it is better known for two things: Being home to the Daley political clan and also to the **US Cellular Field**, where the Chicago White Sox play baseball. Bronzeville was one of the most significant neighborhoods in African-American history. Many of the buildings in the neighborhood were built and financed by African-American capital during the neighborhood's heydey in the early 20th century. After suffering from neglect, the neighborhood is enjoying a resurgence. Nearby Chinatown pales in geographic size to the likes of San Francisco or New York. What the area lacks in physical stature, though, it makes up for in diversity of offerings.

Blues Heaven

2120 S. Michigan Ave. 312-808-1286. www.bluesheaven.com.

The former home to Chess Records Office and Studios is where classic like "Red Rooster" and "Johnny B Goode" were recorded.
Take a tour of this spot, which is now home to Blues Heaven, and you can almost hear legends like Muddy Waters, Willie Dixon and the Rolling Stones in the ether. **Tours** include the main studio and rehearsal spaces.

Chinese-American Museum of Chicago
See p55.
238 W. 23rd St.

Illinois Institute of Technology (IIT)★

3201 S. State St. 312-567-5014. www.iit.edu.

The IIT campus realizes the vision of master Modernist architect **Ludwig Mies van der Rohe** (1886–1969), who directed the school's architecture program after fleeing Nazi Germany. There are a number of worthy buildings on campus. Among those that are not-to-be-missed are **S.R. Crown Hall★★** and **Carr Memorial Chapel**. Crown Hall is the crowning achievement for both Mies van der Rohe and IIT, with its glass-waled pavilion and dramatic flat roof. Carr is the only church ever designed by Mies.
Dutch architect **Rem Koolhaas** continued the tradition in the 21st century with the **McCormick Tribune Campus Center★**.

US Cellular Field

333 W. 35th St. 312-674-1000. whitesox.mlb.com.

The Cubs' **Wrigley Field★** *(see p43)*, gets all the love, but this home to the Chicago White Sox is not a bad place to see a baseball game. The stadium replaced the old Comiskey Park in 1991.
What "The Cell" lacks in charm it makes up for in creature comforts, such as more spacious seating and concession stands that have vegetarian-friendly options.
Plus, the Sox put on an excellent fireworks display after many games.

LAKEVIEW

Bounded by Lake Michigan west to Ashland Ave. and Fullerton Ave. & Irving Park Rd.

Home to **Wrigley Field★**, Belmont Harbor and scores of 20-somethings who have recently moved to Chicago from college towns across the country, Lakeview is one of the most active—and crowded—of the North Side neighborhoods. Come here to enjoy live music, live baseball and 24-7 energy. Just don't drive: Parking is all but impossible!

Hutchinson Street District★
See p72.
Between Lake Shore Dr & Hazel St.

Wrigley Field★
See p43.
1060 W. Addison St.

Southport Avenue
See p104.
Bounded by Belmont Ave. & Irving Park Rd.

HYDE PARK

South of downtown, bounded by Lake Michigan west to Cottage Grove Ave., and 49th St & 60th St.

Best-known as home to the **University of Chicago★★**, Hyde Park is the South Side neighborhood even North Siders love. Whether you are an architecture fan, an academic or a shopper, you'll be able to spend hours here strolling the leafy streets.

Museum of Science and Industry★★★
See pp48, 95.
57th St., at S. Lake Shore Dr.

Oriental Institute★★
See p52.
1155 E. 58th St.

Elijah Muhammad House

4855 S. Woodlawn Ave.

You can't miss the Mediterranean Modern style of this 1971 house, as it is so distinct from the rest of the 19th century style of the area. You also are unlikely to miss it as it will be surrounded by guards, either on foot or in cars, whether you walk by day or night.

The house is home to the Nation of Islam leader, and is under constant watch. Admire the stained-glass windows and red-tiled roof. Across the street you'll see similar, albeit smaller, homes that were built for Muhammad's son.

Robie House★★
See p71.
5757 S. Woodlawn Ave.

LANDMARKS

Chicago has few towering monuments or hallowed spaces. This is a practical city where the most important landmarks are working buildings in busy neighborhoods. Indeed, the city of Chicago has conferred "landmark status" on 203 individual sites and 36 districts, from the Black Metropolis-Bronzeville District on the South Side to the Uptown Theater on the north. Besides these literal landmarks, however, certain icons say "Chicago" around the world.

John Hancock Center★★★

875 N. Michigan Ave.

Muscular and monumental, nothing says Chicago like the profile of "Big John." Built in 1969 (Skidmore, Owings & Merrill), the 100-story tower is a city unto itself, with a 2.8

John Hancock Center

©Chicago Architecture Foundation/Anne Evans

million square feet housing retail, restaurant, office and residential space. These homes were the highest in the world.... until they were "trumped" by the Trump Tower, which, when it opened in 2008 on the north bank of the Chicago River, offered luxury condos that are even higher. The Hancock tower's tapering frame is crisscrossed by brawny braces, which eliminate the need for inner support beams, greatly enlarging the usable space inside. Made of some 46,000 tons of steel, the building can easily withstand gravity and wind. It's lovely at night, when a band of lights girdles the heights of the building in festive holiday color or plain bright white.

Walk around to the west side of the building's base and follow the wide steps down into a large sunken plaza framing colorful planters and a waterfall. From the plaza you'll have interesting views of the surrounding Mag Mile

High-altitude Dining: Signature Room at the 95th

For breathtaking views of the lake and Navy Pier, with food to match, take the elevator up to the Signature Room on the 95th floor *(312-787-9596; www.signatureroom.com)*. The lavish lunch buffet (or you can order off the menu) is a treat, and dinnertime offerings include well-prepared seafood and hearty meat dishes. If you're not up for an expensive dinner, go up one floor to the **Signature Lounge at the 96th** for 360-degree panoramas, a bit of jazz and a specialty martini. Or perhaps a nightcap and dessert. Dress is "upscale casual."

MUST SEE

skyscrapers and a sheltered place to soak up the sun and enjoy a cup of coffee.

The Hancock Observatory

On the 94th floor of the John Hancock Center. 888-875-8439. www.hancock-observatory.com. Open daily 9am–11pm (last ticket sold at 10:45pm). $15 adults, $9 children (free for children under age 4).

During the 39 seconds that the elevator takes to ascend to the 94th floor, your ears will pop and your stomach will drop. Once there, however, the panoramic **views★★★** of lake and landscape in every direction are well worth the ride. On a clear day, you'll see four states: Illinois, Indiana, Wisconsin and Michigan, and, of course, the blue expanse of Lake Michigan that stretches east and north. The open-air **Skywalk**, the highest balcony in America, allows visitors to experience the weather a thousand feet up, regardless of the Chicago weather (prepare for wind). Other attractions, such as a history wall, recorded tours and talking telescopes are fun and informative, but let's face it—it's the view that counts.

Sears Tower★★★

233 S. Wacker Dr.

Tallest building in the world for more than 20 years, this 110-story feat of engineering cuts an unmistakable profile on the city's skyline. At the time of its construction, from 1968 to 1974, the city did not require a zoning variance for the tower, allowing it to rise to an unsurpassed height

of 1,450 feet. Since 1996, the tower has twice been topped as world's tallest building; first by the Petronas Towers in Kuala Lumpur, Malaysia, and in 2003 by Taipei 101 in Taipei, Taiwan. The Sears Tower still holds the title of world's tallest building to the tips of its antennae, and it remains—so far—the tallest building in the US. It may also be the deepest.

Designed by Skidmore, Owings & Merrill, one of the most influential architectural firms of the 20th century, the Sears Tower is composed of nine rectangular tubes resting on more than 100 steel and concrete caissons anchored into the bedrock hundreds of feet below ground. These 75-foot-high bundled tubes provide maximum resistance to high winds; two tubes end at the 50th floor, two at the 66th floor, and three more at the 90th floor. Clad in black aluminum and bronze-tinted glass, the tower's structural skeleton required more than 75,000 tons of steel. Check out the barrel-vaulted entrance on Wacker Drive, where

©Chicago Architecture Foundation/Anne Evans

Sears Tower

LANDMARKS

Chicago's Watermark

Of course, the biggest landmark (watermark, really) in the city spreads out from its doorstep over 22,000 square miles. That would be **Lake Michigan**, and it is an awe-inspiring sight. The name comes from an Algonquian word meaning "big lake," but actually, Michigan is but the third-largest of the five Great Lakes and the only one completely within US borders.

At nearly 1,000 feet at its deepest, the lake never freezes all the way across—a distance of about 30 miles at the southern end. To get a real sense of Lake Michigan, take a walk along the lakefront from Navy Pier to the Museum Campus. The lake's moods change daily, but it is always beautiful.

sculptor Alexander Calder's mobile **The Universe**, a collection of brightly colored forms, turns and twirls. Despite the attraction's popularity, the lines to the top generally move quickly.

Tower Facts
- Even in high wind, the top of the Sears Tower never sways more than six inches.
- The tower weighs in at 222,500 tons, and it's covered by 28 acres of black aluminum.

Buckingham Fountain★★
See p64. Columbus Dr., at Congress Pkwy. in Grant Park.

Marquette Building★★

140 S. Dearborn St. 312-726-8000. www.macfound.org.

The MacArthur Foundation bought and renovated this landmark building and now offers a free exhibit *(Mon–Fri 7am–6pm, Sat–Sun 9 am–6pm)* about this early skyscraper's magnificent details. Highlights include the brick and terracotta ornament and bronze heads of Native American explorers.

Tall Tales

If size matters to you, here's how the Sears Tower and "Big John" stack up:

	Sears	**John Hancock**
Height	1,450 feet without antennae	1,127 feet
Stories	110	100
Weight	222,500 tons	192,000 tons
Square feet	4.5 million	2.8 million
Elevators	103	50
Top elevator speed	1,600 feet per minute	1,800 feet per minute
Number of windows	16,100	11,459
Steps to the top	2,232	1,632

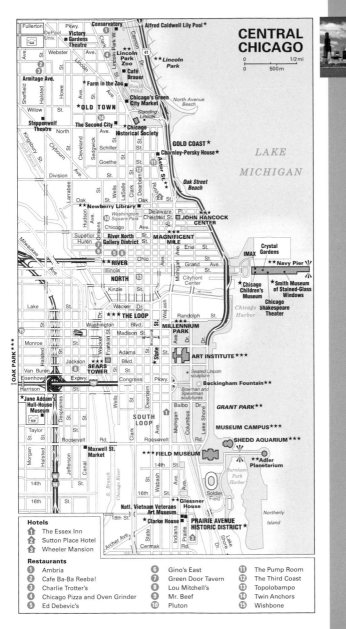

CENTRAL CHICAGO

0   1/2 mi
0   500m

Fullerton Pkwy.
DePaul Univ.
Conservatory ★
Victory Gardens Theatre
★★ Lincoln Park Zoo
Alfred Caldwell Lily Pool ★
Webster Ave.
Clark
Lincoln Park W.
Cannon Dr.
★★ Lincoln Park
Armitage Ave.
Sheffield Ave.
Halsted St.
Howe St.
Lincoln Ave.
Larrabee
Café Brauer ■
South Pond
Farm in the Zoo ■
Willow St.
Chicago's Green City Market
North Avenue Beach
★ OLD TOWN
Steppenwolf Theatre
The Second City ★
Standing Lincoln
North Ave.
Clybourn
Kingsbury
Cleveland
Sedgwick
Wells
LaSalle
Chicago Historical Society ★
Schiller St.
Goethe St.
GOLD COAST ★
Charnley-Persky House ★
Astor St.
LAKE MICHIGAN
Division St.
Larrabee
Canal
Clark
Dearborn
Rush
Oak St.
Oak Street Beach
★★ Newberry Library ■
Hudson
Washington Square Park
Delaware Pl.
Chestnut St.
★★★ JOHN HANCOCK CENTER
Superior St.
Huron St.
Chicago Ave.
Ontario
River North Gallery District
★★★ MAGNIFICENT MILE
Milwaukee Ave.
Erie St.
Ohio St.
Grand Ave.
Michigan Ave.
IMAX
Crystal Gardens
★★ RIVER NORTH
Illinois St.
Cityfront Center
★★ Navy Pier
Kinzie St.
Wacker Dr.
Wabash
Smith Museum of Stained-Glass Windows
★ Chicago Children's Museum
Chicago Harbor
Chicago Shakespeare Theater
Lake St.
★★ THE LOOP
Randolph St.
MILLENNIUM PARK ★★★
OAK PARK ★★★
Washington Blvd.
Madison St.
State St.
Franklin St.
Wacker Dr.
Monroe St.
Adams St.
ART INSTITUTE ★★★
Jackson Blvd.
★★★ SEARS TOWER
Seated Lincoln sculpture
Van Buren St.
Eisenhower Expwy.
Congress Pkwy.
Buckingham Fountain ★★
Bowman and Spearman sculptures
Harrison St.
★ Jane Addams' Hull-House Museum
Desplaines
Halsted St.
Balbo
GRANT PARK ★★
Michigan
Columbus
Lake Shore Dr.
Taylor St.
SOUTH LOOP
MUSEUM CAMPUS ★★★
Roosevelt Rd.
Maxwell St. Market ■
Clark
Canal
Jefferson
Roosevelt Rd.
SHEDD AQUARIUM ★★★
Morgan
Halsted
★★★ FIELD MUSEUM
14th St.
Wabash
Ave.
Burnham Park Harbor
★★ Adler Planetarium
S. Branch Chicago River
16th St.
Soldier Field
Natl. Vietnam Veterans Art Museum ■
★★ Gleasner House
18th St.
Northerly Island
★ Clarke House
PRAIRIE AVENUE HISTORIC DISTRICT ★
Archer Ave.
State St.
Indiana
Prairie
Cermak Rd.
Lake Shore Dr.

Hotels
1. The Essex Inn
2. Sutton Place Hotel
3. Wheeler Mansion

Restaurants
1. Ambria
2. Cafe Ba-Ba-Reeba!
3. Charlie Trotter's
4. Chicago Pizza and Oven Grinder
5. Ed Debevic's
6. Gino's East
7. Green Door Tavern
8. Lou Mitchell's
9. Mr. Beef
10. Pluton
11. The Pump Room
12. The Third Coast
13. Topolobampo
14. Twin Anchors
15. Wishbone

Chicago River Tours

The Chicago River flows backwards from Lake Michigan (engineers reversed its flow in 1900 to keep waste out of the lake, the source of the city's drinking water). The river is now spanned by some 52 movable bridges, each one an engineering marvel. Condos and restaurants line its banks, the pleasant **Riverwalk★** winds along beside it, and great works of urban architecture loom above it.

To enjoy these vistas, take a Chicago Architecture Foundation **Architecture River Cruise**. The 90-minute tours depart at least six times daily, rain or shine, from May 1 to the end of November from the dock located at the southeast corner of the Michigan Avenue Bridge and Wacker Drive *(reservations recommended: 312-902-1500; for details, contact the Architecture Foundation: 312-922-3432 or www.architecture.org).*

Chicago Water Tower
©Chicago Architecture Foundation/Anne Evans

feet) was built on land and floated out to be firmly grounded into the lake bottom at a depth of 40 feet. (From the shoreline, you can see the original crib's successors up and down the lakefront.) A tunnel was then built 6 feet under the lakebed to connect the crib with the pumping station and provide the city with fresh water from the lake. Ridiculed by naysayers, the plan came to be recognized as a masterpiece of engineering. Now dwarfed by high rises, the castle-like structures of the Chicago Water Tower and

Navy Pier★★

See pp15, 87, 97. 600 E. Grand Ave., at Lake Michigan.

Chicago Water Tower and Pumping Station★

On either side of N. Michigan Ave., at Chicago Ave.

In 1850s Chicago, contaminated water took its toll on human health and city development. In 1855 city sewage commissioners decided to bring in fresh lake water by building a tunnel extending two miles out under Lake Michigan. A huge water intake "crib" (50 feet by 70

Billy Goat's Curse

It started when William Sianis and his billy goat, Murphy, were ejected from Game 4 of the World Series at Wrigley Field in 1945. "Cubs, they not gonna win anymore," Sianis vowed. The team lost the series and never returned.

Though attempts have been made to lift the curse by allowing Murphy's descendants into Wrigley, it endures. As does Sianis' **Billy Goat Tavern** *(430 N. Michigan Ave., lower level; 312-222-1525).*

The subterranean tavern (now run by Sianis' nephew, Sam) offers a real, greasy slice of Chicago history.

Pumping Station (built in the late 1860s) were the only two public buildings to survive the 1871 fire. Today a lovely park surrounds the tower, while the pumping station, though still operational, has been refitted as the home of **Lookingglass Theatre** *(312-337-0665; www.lookingglasstheatre.org)*. The building is a frequent meeting place for Mag Mile tourists.

Wrigley Field★

1060 W. Addison St. 773-404-2827. www.chicago.cubs.com. For ticket information, see p89.

Built as Weeghman Field in 1914 for the Chicago Whales of the Federal League before being occupied by the Cubs of the National League two years later, this stadium is an icon for baseball lovers everywhere. It's the oldest surviving National League ballpark and second only to Boston's Fenway Park (1912) overall. The Chicago Bears played football here from their beginnings in 1921 until 1970 before moving to Soldier Field in 1971. Famous for its ivy walls and lovable losing

teams, the stadium is surrounded by early 20th century flats rather than the usual sea of parking lots. Many of the adjacent buildings boast rooftop clubs where ticket buyers watch the game over the outfield walls. The first night game was played here in 1988 after a long battle with neighbors to keep lights out of the field.
Current talk includes moving Wrigley's walls out ten feet—is nothing sacred?

Skydeck

Enter on Jackson Blvd., between Wacker Dr. & Franklin St. 312-875-9696. www.theskydeck.com. Open May–Sept 10am–10pm. Rest of the year 10am–8pm. $12.25 adults, $9.50 children.

Elevators blast off to the top of the Sears Tower at 1,600 feet per minute. When you land on the Skydeck, 103 stories up, an awesome **view★★★** (on a clear day) for 50 miles around greets you. Interactive exhibits, telescopes and kid-level views help you pick out sites 1,353 feet below, from lakeshores to railroads to rooftops.

City of Chicago/Chris McGuire

Wrigley Field

MUSEUMS

Chicago takes justifiable pride in its array of museums; indeed, you could spend a week and not do them all justice. Some command majestic profiles on the lakefront; others grace parks and neighborhoods around the city. From earthly fossils to celestial bodies, Chicago's museums can indulge most any cultural pleasure.

Modern Wing, The Art Institute of Chicago

© The Art Institute of Chicago

Art Institute of Chicago★★★

111 S. Michigan Ave. 312-443-3600. www.artinstituteofchicago.org. Open year-round Mon–Fri 10:30am–4:30pm (Thu free from 5pm until 8pm), Sat–Sun 10am–5pm. Closed Thanksgiving Day, Christmas Day and New Year's Day. $12 adults; $7 children (free for children ages 12 and under). Free admission during the summer: Thu–Fri, 5pm–9pm.

One of the great museums of the world and the preeminent arts institution of the Midwest, the Art Institute of Chicago (AIC) is a comprehensive center for arts education and exhibition. Its collections span 5,000 years and draw on the cultures of Europe, Asia, Africa and the Americas. If you're a lover of the Impressionist period, this is the place for you: the museum's reputation rests primarily on its

Eat Your Art Out

For a quick sandwich, grill selection, pizza or salad (and best for kids), visit the self-service **Café** on the lower level. The **Garden Restaurant** *(lower level; 312-553-9675)* features table service, a full bar, and a menu of contemporary American and seafood dishes. During the summer, the restaurant flings wide its doors onto the shady McKinlock Court for alfresco dining. Enter at Columbus Drive if you are only dining.

collection of Impressionist and post-Impressionist paintings, one of the largest and most important outside France. Immerse yourself in a gallery or two, or sample a variety of the institute's visual delights. Founded as one of the first art schools in the US in 1866 (the School of the Art Institute remains a world-class facility), the

AIC was reorganized to include a museum in 1879. The grand **World's Columbian Exposition** of 1893 provided the perfect opportunity for trustees to construct the glorious temple of art that stands on Michigan Avenue today, guarded by the bronze lions cast by sculptor Edward Kemeys in 1894. From the 50,000 square feet of the original Allerton Building, the institute has expanded to encompass more than 400,000 square feet, spanning the block between Michigan Avenue and Columbus Drive.

A new, $300-million Modern Wing designed by Renzo Piano is slated to add another 65,000 square feet of gallery space on the building's north side by May 2009.

Heart of the Art Institute

European Painting and Sculpture★★ – Medieval, Renaissance, and Baroque masterpieces occupy the entire second floor of the Allerton Building. They trace the development of Western painting from flat medieval landscapes to the flamboyance of

A Sunday on La Grand Jatte - 1884 (1884-86) by Georges Seurat

Photo ©The Art Institute of Chicago, Helen Birch Bartlett Memorial Collection

MUSEUMS

45

the Rococo. Don't miss works by Botticelli, Rembrandt and El Greco.

19th century European Painting★★★
– From Goya to Gauguin, these galleries in upper Gunsaulus Hall sparkle with painterly genius. Check out the breathtaking array of Impressionists and Post-Impressionist iconic masterpieces by Seurat, Monet, van Gogh, Toulouse-Lautrec, and more. This collection was freshly reinstalled summer 2008.

The Modern Wing★★
– The new galleries in the Modern Wing houses the collections of modern art, contemporary art, photography, and architecture and design. This is the largest expansion in the Art Institute's history, showcasing as never before the museum's commitment to emerging art, new technology, and modernity. Opens to the public May 16, 2009.

American Art★★
– Beginning with a delightful gallery of folk art, these exhibits chronicle the development of American taste through furniture, decorative arts, paintings and sculpture. Iconic masterpieces such as Grant Wood's American Gothic and Edward Hopper's Nighthawks can be found in this recently reinstalled presentation of the collection.

European Decorative Arts★★
– This collection is a trove of household, decorative and religious objects produced since AD 1100. Check out the delectable **Rubloff Paperweight Collection★**, which looks good enough to eat.

Asian Art★★★
– In addition to a stunning collection of Chinese, Japanese, and Korean ancient artifacts, visitors should stroll through the Alsdorf Galleries of Indian and Southeast Asian Sculptures—a newly reinstalled, daylit space with an amazing view of the Chicago skyline.

Field Museum of Natural History★★★

1400 S. Lake Shore Dr. 312-922-9410. www.fieldmuseum.org. Open year-round daily 9am–5pm (last entry 4pm). Closed Dec 25. $22 adults, $12 children ages 4–11 (free for children 3 and under). Admission is discounted for Chicago residents.

This world-class natural history institution occupies a suitably grand place at the south end of Grant Park. Known as the **Museum**

Campus★★★, this area also includes the **Shedd Aquarium★★★** and the **Adler Planetarium★★**. Nine acres of exhibit halls and over 20 million artifacts await you in the temple-like building completed in 1921 by architect Daniel Burnham. Dinosaur bones, artifacts from cultures around the world and animal taxidermy have all been incorporated into fun, modern exhibits, though some galleries await updating. Even if only four percent of the collections are on exhibit when you go, there's still plenty to see!

A Dino Named Sue★★ –

The museum's famous *Tyrannosaurus rex* skeleton occupies the place of honor on the main floor in Stanley Field Hall.
You can't miss Sue—she's 13 feet tall at the hip with a menacing grin! For more on Sue and her ilk, visit the second-floor galleries just above her. There you'll be able to get a close look at her actual skull, which, weighing in at 600 pounds, is too heavy to display on the skeleton.

Outstanding in the Field

Africa★★– This kaleidoscopic exhibit ventures from the streets of Dakar, Senegal, to the sand dunes of the Sahara. The sweeping presentation investigates African politics, art, environment, wildlife, commerce and family life by highlighting the diverse cultures of the continent.

Eskimos and Northwest Coast Indians★★ – A seemingly endless display of masks, totem poles, articles of clothing and other Native American artifacts contrasts life in the Arctic and the Northwest.

Dino Zone★★ – At this exhibit you can touch dinosaur bones and teeth, and test your knowledge of dino trivia. The exhibit incorporates the newest scientific research about early life on earth. There is a hands-on interpretive station and in the McDonald's Fossil Preparation Lab, you can watch fossils being prepared.

Hall of Gems★ – All love these shimmering precious and semiprecious stones, lusciously illuminated in a small darkened space.

Tyrannosaurus rex, "Sue"

© The Field Museum

MUSEUMS

Touring Tip: Visiting MSI

This can be a hard museum to navigate efficiently because of its size and layout. Grab a floor plan and purchase entry, special-exhibit and **Omnimax** tickets as you enter the Great Hall from the underground garage. Plan to see the **Coal Mine★★**, **Idea Factory** and **U-505 Submarine★** early, as lines for these can develop fast. In the Great Hall, you can check your coat and rent a stroller before you ascend the escalator, elevators or stairs to the ground level. Exhibits, restrooms and a cafeteria can be found on this floor. From here, the museum complex takes in the **Henry Crown Space Center** and three floors within the central, east and west pavilions. The floors are connected by four color-coded stairwells off the rotunda of the central pavilion. East of the central pavilion, the Crown Center connects to the pavilions by a hallway accessible from the ground floor.

Nature Walk★ – The specimens and dioramas at the Field are second to none; they take you on a trek through woods, wetlands and other wild places.

Plants of the World★ – This display will dazzle you with the incredible variety of form, color and function of the world's plants.

Traveling the Pacific★ and **Pacific Spirits★** – These adjacent exhibits showcase the museum's collections from the cultures of the South Pacific. The highlight is the 1881 **Maori meeting house**, moved from New Zealand and reconstructed here piece by piece.

Underground Adventure★ – *Extra charge.* Walk among the creepy crawlies that live beneath our feet (simulated, of course) and get a bug's-eye view of life in the dirt.

Museum of Science and Industry★★★

57th St., at S. Lake Shore Dr. 773-684-1414. www.msichicago. org. Open year-round Memorial Day–Labor Day Mon–Sat 9:30am–5:30pm, Sun 11am–5:30pm; rest of the year Mon–Sat 9:30am–4pm, Sun 11am–4pm. Closed Dec 25. $13 adults, $9 children (ages 3–11). Free admission days vary by season. Additional charge for Omnimax Theater & special exhibits.

U-505 Submarine, Museum of Science and Industry

MUST SEE

Scott Brownell/Museum of Science and Industry

This noisy hall of wonders and widgets is one of Chicago's most popular attractions, and the crowds prove it. Since 1933, the "MSI" has occupied the only building left standing after the **World's Columbian Exposition** of 1893 *(see p67)*. Designed in the grand classical style by Charles B. Atwood as the Palace of Fine Arts (now the **Museum of Science and Industry★★★**), the building fell into disrepair until 1926 when the idea to house an "industrial" museum there took root. Over the years the museum has collected an amazing array of oddities and artifacts—from a miniature **Fairy Castle★** to the world's fastest car. Today, spread out over four floors, the MSI covers topics in transportation, the human body, technology and manufacturing, communication, energy and environment, and space and defense. *For a description of exhibits, see p95.*

Shedd Aquarium★★★

1200 S. Lake Shore Dr. 312-559-0200. www.shedd.org. Open Mon-Fri 9am–5pm. Sat–Sun 9am–6pm. Closed Dec 25. All-access pass: $24.95 adults, $17.95 children (ages 3–11). Admission is discounted for Chicago residents.

Hard by Lake Michigan, the Shedd Aquarium brings the ocean to the lakefront. As the world's largest indoor aquarium, it houses aquatic creatures from around the globe—from tiny, jewel-like spiny lobsters to 1,500-pound beluga whales. The Shedd's exhibits and programs emphasize conservation and the environment, and its remarkable animals bring the message vividly to life. The building opened in 1930 and resembles a

---

Touring Tip

Arrive early when you visit this popular attraction; it gets especially crowded during the summer and on weekends. Plan your visit for Sunday morning if you really want to avoid the lines. To save a few bucks, go for the Shedd's **Discount Days** on Monday and Tuesday from mid-September to the end of February. On these days, general admission is free and admission to the Oceanarium and Wild Reef exhibits is offered at a discount *($15 adults, $10 children)*.

Underwater exploration at Shedd Aquarium

©Edward Lines/Shedd Aquarium

MUSEUMS

Best of the Beasts

Of course you won't want to miss the dolphins, whales and sharks, but don't overlook some of the less obvious aquatic wonders at the Shedd. Our favorites include **Nickel** the Lucky Sea Turtle, who lives in the Caribbean Reef tank. You'll know her by her "limp," a reminder of injuries from which she is recovering. The name? During her rehab, vets found a nickel lodged in her throat. And be sure to pay your respects to Granddad, the 80-year-old lungfish who arrived at the aquarium as a youngster in 1933. Oh, and those green things you see in many habitats? They're heads of romaine lettuce—a favorite treat among certain residents.

monument to the Roman sea god, Neptune, whose trident tops the roof. Inside, keep an eye out for decorative wave and shell patterns and charming sea creatures that crawl over light fixtures, tiles and doorways. A pioneer at re-creating aquatic habitats, the Shedd has transformed many of its older exhibits into mini-ecosystems that support not only fish but plants, birds and a furry surprise or two.

Dive In!

When you buy your admission ticket, you'll receive a schedule of feedings, demonstrations and shows for that day.

Oceanarium★★ – This amazing habitat re-creates a Pacific Northwest ecosystem. Stroll "along the coast," following the edge of the oversized pools where beluga whales, Pacific white-sided dolphins and harbor seals carouse. The wide expanse of

Lake Michigan stretches beyond, a vista barely interrupted by the oceanarium's glass wall. Beneath the pools, underwater-viewing galleries bring you nose to snout with graceful dolphins. And be prepared to laugh at the penguin habitat, where beguiling rockhoppers, magellenics and gentoos go about their business, diving, swimming and waddling.

Wild Reef★★ – This extraordinary exhibit takes you deep into a Philippine coral reef to see one of the world's most diverse habitats. Displays explain the life cycle of the reef and illustrate how living corals form, survive and die. A huge wall of water teeming with gemlike fish against a backdrop of artificial coral bends around the space. See sharks up close and personal in the impressive tank around the corner, and watch underfoot to see little stingrays darting and gliding. So as not to harvest coral from the wild,

No Silly Animal Tricks

Shedd animal behaviorists are adamant about the motive behind the Marine Mammal Presentations. The behaviors you'll see reflect natural activities in the wild. A spyhopping dolphin, for instance, stands straight up on its tail for a better view above the water. The animals are also taught certain behaviors to make medical exams easier. *Oceanarium shows are held daily 10:30am, 11:30am, 1:30pm & 3:30pm; with an extra 4:30pm show on weekends.*

©Shedd Aquarium

Caribbean Reef, Shedd Aquarium

the Shedd grows (or fabricates) its own. Wild Reef offers excellent narrated dives at 10.30am.

Amazon Rising: Seasons of the River★ – In these galleries you'll experience a year in the life of an Amazon floodplain forest. Habitats are stocked with some 250 species, including a huge anaconda and a tiny pigmy marmoset.

Caribbean Reef★ – If you stare long enough into these 90,000 gallons of fishy fun, you might spot all of the 500 tropical fish that live there, including hammerhead sharks, rays, and a sea turtle named Nickel *(see box, opposite page)*. Stick around for feeding time, which happens five times a day.

Adler Planetarium★★

1300 S. Lake shore Dr. 312-922-7827. www.adlerplanetarium. org. Open daily 9:30am–4:30pm, first Friday every other month 9am–10pm. Closed Thanksgiving Day & Dec 25. $23 adults, $19 children (ages 4–17); fee includes admission and two sky shows.

It's worth the **views★★** up and down the lakefront to walk out to the Adler, which occupies a beautiful setting. The oldest planetarium in the Western Hemisphere, it is also renowned

Museum Campus Eats

You have plenty of choices for lunch at Museum Campus visit. Enjoy fresh sandwiches (or take a coffee break) in the shadow of Sue the T-rex at the Field Museum's **Corner Bakery**. (If the kids vote for **McDonald's**, you'll find it in the basement.) Visit the **Bubble Net Food Court** at the Shedd Aquarium for pizza, burgers and the like. For the only table service on the Museum Campus, try **Soundings Restaurant** at the Shedd Aquarium. The menu features gourmet sandwiches, soups—and, yes, seafood—wine and cocktails in an attractive dining room overlooking the lake *(if you wish to dine but not visit the aquarium, reservations are required: 312-692-3277)*. **Galileo Café** at the Adler Planetarium offers cafeteria-style sandwiches, salads and soups as well as a stunning view. Or bring your own picnic supplies and dine *al fresco* on the campus grounds in summer.

MUSEUMS

Touring Tip

You'll want to leave some time to explore the rest of the museum as well, which can be a challenge to figure out because of the shape of the space (be sure to pick up a floor plan at the admissions desk). On the upper level, interactive exhibits attempt to demystify the universe, the Milky Way galaxy and our solar system. Lower-level exhibits journey through the history of Western astronomy as well as the importance of sky study to ancient cultures.

for its fine collection of historic astronomical instruments and its splendid sky shows.

Chicago's planetarium sprang from philanthropist Max Adler's belief that a Zeiss projector (used for re-creating the night sky on an enclosed dome) would be a great teaching tool for the city. He donated $1 million, and architect Ernest A. Grunsfeld Jr. designed a compact, red-granite jewel for the dramatic setting at the tip of Northerly Island. A major renovation in 1999 added 60,000 square feet of exhibit space that enclosed two-thirds of the old Art Deco building in glass. As you make your way through the new space, note the charming bronze signs of the zodiac that still adorn each corner of the original 12-sided structure.

The Sky's the Limit

StarRider® Theater★★ – Located on the lower level, "the world's first interactive computer-graphics theater" immerses you in the stars on its domed screen. Here you'll voyage through the universe, land on Mars or visit the tombs and temples of ancient Egypt.

History of Astronomy Gallery★ – *Lower level*. This gallery showcases the planetarium's extensive collection of curious historic instruments for measuring time, earth and space.

If more modern space exploration suits your taste, visit **CyberSpace**, where news about the latest Mars landings and space-probe discoveries are broadcast at VisionStations. The Adler hosts many topical events throughout the year. Check schedules for special lectures and educational sessions.

Adler Planetarium

University of Chicago★★

From 55th St. on the north to 60th St. on the south, between Dorchester &
Maryland Aves. The main quad lies along 58th St., between Ellis & University Aves.
This handsome 190-acre urban campus is steeped in history, reputation and,
well, Nobel Prizes (78 have been awarded to students, researchers and faculty—
more than any other school). Founded in 1890 with a strong academic vision,
the U of C blossomed early into one of the nation's leading research schools. In
the early 1940s, the abandoned football grandstands concealed the Manhattan
Project laboratory of Enrico Fermi, whose team of physicists achieved the first
self-sustaining nuclear reaction. Immerse yourself in collegiate atmosphere with
lunch at **Medici** *(1327 E. 57th St.; 773-667-7394)*, where students have gathered to
eat pizza and burgers for decades.

Oriental Institute★★

1155 E. 58th St., at University
Ave., on the University of Chicago
campus. 773-702-9514.
www.oi.uchicago.edu. Open year-
round Tue–Sat 10am–6pm (Wed
until 8:30pm), Sun noon–6pm.
Closed major holidays.

Oriental Institute

©Oriental Institute, University of Chicago

While the institute is dedicated
to the study of languages, history
and cultures of the ancient Near
East, its museum contains one of
the world's choicest collections of
Near Eastern art and antiquities.
Most of its 75,000 artifacts were
collected by institute arche-
ologists, including James Henry
Breasted, who led the University
of Chicago's first field expedition
to the land we now know as Iraq
in 1904 and created the institute
in 1919.

The institute has resided in its
current building on the University
of Chicago campus since 1931.
The museum galleries have been
undergoing extensive renovation
over the past few years; so far
only the **Egyptian, Mesopota-**
mian and **Persian** exhibits have
reopened.

Don't miss the gift shop, which
sells better-than-average museum
shop fare, including quality jewelry.

Lunch at Big Shoulders

312-587-7766. Light and healthy
lunches (including children's spe-
cials) compete with great views
of Lincoln Park in this café, set in a
two-story glass-enclosed turret at
the Chicago History Museum.
Notice the re-creation of the massive archway framing the inside
doorway; it once marked the entrance to the Union Stockyards,
site of Chicago's infamous slaugh-
terhouses in the 19th century.

MUSEUMS

53

Puck's

On the east side of the Museum of Contemporary Art. Overlooking the sculpture garden and Lake Michigan beyond through an expansive glass wall, Puck's features fine dining with a view. The menu highlights Wolfgang Puck's signature Chinois chicken salad and a selection of specialty pizzas along with salads and sandwiches *(reservations recommended; 312-397-4034; www.mcachicago.org).*

Chicago History Museum★

1601 N. Clark St., at North Ave. 312-642-4600. www.chicagohs. org. Open year-round Mon–Sat 9:30am–4:30pm (Thu until 8pm), Sun noon–5pm. Closed Jan 1, Thanksgiving Day & Dec 25. $14 with audio tours (ages 12 and under free). Free Mon.

Want to delve deeper into Chicago's past? Then don't miss a visit to the Chicago History Museum, located at the southwestern corner of Lincoln Park. Organized in 1856, the city's oldest cultural institution covers America until 1865 and Chicago since the first explorers. Its collections are chock-full of documents and objects connected to Chicago's first settlers, as well as historic photographs, memorabilia from Chicago's two world's fairs, and, of course, the Chicago Fire.

Museum of Contemporary Art★

220 E. Chicago Ave. 312-280-2660. www.mcachicago.org. Open year-round Wed–Sun 10am–5pm (Tue until 8pm). Closed Jan 1, Thanksgiving Day & Dec 25. $10 (ages 12 and under free). Free Tue.

The task of presenting the avant-garde can be daunting, but the MCA does a good job of making the works and movements of the art of our time accessible to everyone through thoughtful label writing, audio programming and free guided tours *(check schedule at desk).* Exhibits mounted on a rotating basis from the museum's 7,000-piece permanent collection generally occupy the third- and fourth-floor galleries. Much of what you'll see focuses on new acquisitions and works by living artists, but the museum's collection also includes the art of Marcel Duchamp, Max Ernst, René Magritte, Alexander Calder, Andy Warhol and a host of Chicago and Illinois artists such as Ed Paschke, June Leaf and Jim Nutt.

The MCA staff are excellent event planners. If you are traveling with kids, find out if you'll be in town during Family Day, periodic Saturdays when the whole family (including the dog) is welcome for free, hands-on programming.

©Hedrich Blessing/Museum of Contemporary Art

Museum of Contemporary Art

Smart Museum of Art★

5550 S. Greenwood Ave., on the University of Chicago campus. 773-702-0200. www.smartmuseum. uchicago.edu. Open mid-Jun–mid-Sept Tue–Fri 10am–4pm, weekends 11am–5pm. Rest of the year Tue, Wed & Fri 10am–4pm, Thu 10am–8pm, weekends 11am–5pm. Galleries closed major holidays.

Opened in 1974 and named for the founders of *Esquire* magazine, this small jewel of a university museum holds 7,500 pieces spanning 5,000 years. The Smart Museum rotates its permanent collection, which excels in arts of the late 19th century and early 20th century, among its four major galleries.

Chinese-American Museum of Chicago

238 W. 23rd St. 312-949-1000. www.ccamuseum.org. Open Fri 9:30am–1:30pm. Sat–Sun 10am–5pm. $2 adults, $1 children.

This relatively new museum in Chinatown features a rotating schedule of temporary exhibits, illuminating the Chinese-American experience, particularly in the Midwest. Previous exhibits have included a look at Chinese immigration and the Great Lakes, toys and games and leisure activities of Chinese-American immigrants. In addition to its exhibition space, the museum offers an excellent resource for those wanting to do research on the Midwestern Chinese-American experience. The museum hosts a number of lecture and other community events throughout the year.

DuSable Museum of African American History

740 E. 56th Pl. 773-947-0600. www.dusablemuseum.org. Open year-round Mon–Sat 10am–5pm, Sun noon–5pm. Closed Mon Jun–Dec, Jan 1, Thanksgiving Day & Dec 25. $3. Free Sun.

Founded in 1961 by Dr. Margaret Goss Burroughs in her home, this cultural and historical museum now occupies a former park administration building. The modern Harold Washington Wing, added to the structure's south side in 1992, houses cultural programs that supplement permanent and traveling exhibits on African-American life, art and history.

Dining with the Prairie School

Tucked away in Lincoln Park, just a short way north of the nature museum, sits a romantic little restaurant **North Pond** *(2610 N. Cannon Dr.; 773-477-5845; www.northpondrestaurant.com)*. Once a skaters' warming hut on the edge of North Pond, the building still serves as a cozy retreat from winter's chill, as well as a cool oasis in summer. Beautifully renovated in Prairie style with warm oak, copper and art-glass accents, the space now houses an elegant eatery that features local and regional ingredients and wines from small American vineyards. Tall windows look out over the pond, the park and the city skyline, and a fieldstone fireplace completes the ambience. Be sure to reserve a table in the front room if you wish to dine with the best view and near a roaring fire in winter.

MUSEUMS

There is also a Community Gallery where artists can exhibit works related to the subjects of the museum.

International Museum of Surgical Science

1524 N. Lake Shore Dr.
312-642-6502. www.imss.org.
Open May–Sept, Tue–Sun
10am–4pm, Oct–Apr, Tue–Sat
10am–4pm. $9 adults, $5 students
and seniors. Free on Tue.

Not for the art snob, the International Museum of Surgical Science offers quirky fun for the curious in the Gold Coast. This 1917 French chateau-style building has four floors, jam-packed with all manner of medical miracles. Check out the ephemera of both Eastern and Western healing practices, ranging from weird-looking apparatus (including an iron lung) and instruments to fine art about medicine, not to mention details about all kinds of odd illnesses.

The Hall of Murals is just as its name suggests: a room devoted to the topic at hand created by Italian painter Gregorio Calvi di Bergolo (1904–1994). While the museum takes a fairly erudite approach to its mission, the collections are still not for those made queasy by science.

Intuit: The Center for Intuitive and Outsider Art

756 N. Milwaukee Ave.,
312-243-9088, www.art.org.
Open Tue–Sat 11am–5pm,
Thu 11am–7:30pm.
Free.

Chicago has countless lesser-known gems, many of which overshadow the Sears Tower in terms of cultural experience. But of all the overlooked cultural institutions, perhaps the most significant is Intuit, the country's leading institution to highlight unschooled folk art, housed just north of downtown.

Officially, Intuit defines its brand of "intuitive and outsider art" as the "work of artists who demonstrate little influence from the mainstream art world and who seem instead motivated by their unique personal visions." Outsider art can also be called "art brut", non-traditional folk art, self-taught art, and visionary art. The museum's permanent collection includes works by Henry Darger, perhaps the best known of all the outside artists. Darger worked as a janitor in Chicago, and his drawings and paintings only brought him fame after his death in 1973.

Intuit is now home to many of the drawings, books and furnishing from his one-room apartment. Other artists in the collection include sculptor James "Son" Thomas, and sharecropper's son S.L. Jones. Temporary exhibitions and special events continue the efforts to educate the world on self-taught artists.

No matter what, don't skip the museum's sculpture garden.

Leather Archives and Museum

6418 N. Greenview Ave. 773-761-9200. www.leather archives.org. Open Thu, Fri noon–8pm, Sat–Sun noon–5pm. $5.

Strictly for grown-ups! For those who are curious, and not traveling with kids, these two buildings can entertain and inform. The museum collection includes shirts, posters, banners and other accoutrements of the leather fetish and sadomasochism world. The collection includes some of the largest assembly of original Etienne works, photos, sexual devices and other related materials. There is also a research library for those whose interest in the sexually charged topic is more academic.

McCormick Tribune Freedom Museum

445 N. Michigan Ave., 312-222-4860, www.freedom museum.us. Open Wed–Mon 10am–6pm. Closed Thanksgiving, Christmas and New Year's Day. Free.

The thought-provoking McCormick Tribune Freedom Museum, located in the Tribune Tower, is the first museum in the country dedicated to the First Amendment. Here you and your family can take in a variety of exhibits that are sure to give you something to discuss on the ride home. Topical exhibits include covering presidential elections, while ongoing exhibits discuss the role the First Amendment has in our daily lives, and the struggles involved in gaining freedom in the USA

dramatic two-story sculpture includes quotes from "everyday people" with their thoughts on freedom. Videos and quizzes on the First Amendment and freedom round-out the offerings.

Mitchell Museum of the American Indian

3001 Central St., Evanston. 847-475-1030. www.mitchell museum.org. Open Tue–Sat 10am–5pm (Thu until 8pm), Sun noon–4pm. $5 adults, $2.50 children, $10 for a family.

This extraordinarily kid-friendly museum is the only one in the area dedicated to the Native American experience. Its collection includes artifacts and artworks that are part of Native American history, but also are put of the community today. Works cover from the Paleo-Indian period to modern day, and tribes from the North American Indian and Inuit people. The museum hosts ongoing hands-on events and exhibits, so kids (and grown-ups) can make headdresses, learn Native American dance, and see how the traditions of the indigenous community is still part of Midwestern culture today.

Museum of Contemporary Photography

600 N. Michigan Ave. 312-663-5554. www.mocp.org. Open Mon–Sat 10am–5pm, Thu 10am–8pm, Sun noon–5pm. Free.

Housed on the campus of Columbia College Chicago, this photography museum is more

Dia de los Muertos

Day of the Dead (celebrated from October 31 to November 2) is a time of great festivity in Mexico, and it's a lot of fun at the National Museum of Mexican Art, too. A blend of ancient Aztec and Christian rituals, including feasting, parades, and the building of colorful home altars, the holiday honors the spirits of those who have died. Women bake skeleton-shaped bread, and children crave *calaveras*, grinning candy skulls. Families visit and decorate cemeteries, singing and dancing as a way of scorning death. The museum celebrates the season annually with demonstrations, programs and an exhibition of Day of the Dead crafts—incorporating symbols such as skulls, skeletons and marigolds.

than a mere academic effort. With more than 8,500 photographs in its permanent collection, MoCP is the place to go in the Midwest to see the work of the best American photographers since 1936. Highlights of the collection include the works of Ansel Adams, Diane Arbus and Jim Dine. The Midwest Photographers Project is a rotating collection that are on loan to the museum for two years. In addition to the artworks, the museum has lightboxes and sculpture.

Museum of Holography

1134 W. Washington Blvd. 312-226-1007. Open Wed–Sun. 12:30pm–5pm. $4.

This quirky museum seems tiny in comparison to the Art Institutes of the world. And, in our digital age, holography is not the mindbender it used to be. But this West Loop institution packs a lot into its small space, so there is more than you can imagine. The holographs here are sophisticated and likely to change any preconceived notions about the technology. Also exhibited is information on holographs used for the medical profession.

National American Italian Sports Hall of Fame

1431 W. Taylor St., 312-226-5566, www.niashf.org. Open Mon–Fri 9am–5pm, Sat–Sun 11am–4pm.

Nestled in Little Italy (where else?), the hall honors the athletes of Italian descent, a surprisingly varied group. In the first-floor Tommy and Jo Lasorda Exhibit Gallery you'll find mementos including Mario Andretti's Indy 500 racecar, Rocky Marciano's World Heavyweight Championship Belt, and Vince Lombardi's last coat worn as coach of the Green Bay Packers.
The artifacts are accompanied by video and audio clips.
Don't miss the sculpture of Joe DiMaggio in the pretty plaza across the street.

National Museum of Mexican Art

1852 W. 19th St. 312-738-1503. www.nationalmuseumofmexican art.org. Open year-round Tue–Sun 10am–5pm (Wed until 8pm). Closed major holidays.

The largest institution of its kind in the US, this respected

MUST SEE

ethnic center is best known for its exhibits and programs focusing on Mexico's colorful celebration of the Day of the Dead *(see box, left)*. A 33,000-square-foot addition enables the museum to exhibit works from its permanent collection in **Mexicanidad: Our Past Is Present**, which journeys from prehistory to the present. Note the stunning beaded mural called *New Awakening*. A new three-year initiative will examine the topic of immigration through different art exhibits, lectures and other programs.

Peggy Notebaert Nature Museum★

2430 N. Cannon Dr. 773-755-5100. www.nature museum.org. Open year-round Mon–Fri 9am–4:30pm, Sat–Sun 10am–5pm. Closed Jan 1, Thanksgiving Day & Dec 25. $7 adults, $4 children (ages 3–12). Free Thu.

Beautifully sited on Lincoln Park, along the lower end of North Pond, this sand-colored "cluster of wedge-shaped blocks" was designed to resemble the sand dunes that once covered this area. Opened in 1999, the museum aims to help visitors "think green" through environmental learning and an appreciation of our dwindling natural resources. Inside, six permanent exhibits fill two levels; outside, pathways wind through native plantings.

Butterfly Haven★ – The air on the second floor is aflutter with 70 species of butterflies, many so beautiful you may mistake them for flowers. Watch out: one of the residents might just hitch a ride on your shoulder! Check out the chrysalis case and talk to the interpreter. If a chrysalis is hatching while you're visiting, you'll be spellbound by the process.

Wilderness Walk – Ants and other live bugs and creatures, along with walk-through dioramas, help you to picture the sand dunes, prairies and savannas native to the greater Chicago area.

RiverWorks – To get the low-down on the Chicago River and other similar waterways, visit this

Peggy Notebaert Nature Museum

first-floor exhibit, where you—and the kids—can splash around and create dams, locks, runoffs and even sewers.

Polish Museum of America

984 N. Milwaukee Ave, 773-384-3352. www.polishmuseum ofamerica.org. Fri–Wed 11am–4pm. $5 adults, $3 children.

The Polish immigrant population is one of Chicago's largest and most proud. This neighborhood museum, in the heart of what was once the epicenter of the local Polish community, is a look at the Polish-American museum. On display are artworks by Polish artists, folk art and costumes and space devoted to that icon of Polish decent: the late Pope John Paul II.
Some people believe that the museum may be haunted by the ghost of Polish composer Ignacy Jan Paderewski.

Smith Museum of Stained-Glass Windows

On Navy Pier, 600 E. Grand Ave. at Lake Michigan. 312-595-5024. Open year-round Mon–Thu 10am–8pm, Fri & Sat 10am–10pm, Sun 10am–7pm.

Filling a series of galleries along the lower-level terraces of Festival Hall, this unique museum showcases more than 100 stained-glass windows from 1897 to the present, all works of art in themselves. Their creators include well-known names such as Louis Comfort Tiffany and John LaFarge, as well as Chicago artists Ed Paschke and Roger Brown.

Spertus Museum

610 S. Michigan Ave. 312-322-1700. www.spertus.edu/ museum. Sun–Wed 10am–5pm, Thu 10am–6pm, Fri 10am–3pm. $7 adults, $5 children, Free Tue 10am–noon and Thu 2pm–6pm.

Housed at the Spertus Institute of Jewish Studies, the museum expanded thanks to the new Spertus building which opened in late 2007. Housed on three floors, the museum has more than 15,000 pieces of Jewish ephemera on display, along with topical permanent and traveling exhibitions relating to Jewish themes. If you are traveling with kids, do not skip the Gray Children's Center, which is appropriate for kids up to age 12. In addition to a number of performances, the center gives kids the space to climb and play, learn language and hear stories relating to Jewish life.
Spertus is known for its thought-provoking public programs. The new facility is home to one of the few kosher eateries in the downtown area as well as a terrific gift shop.

McCormick Tribune Bridgehouse and Chicago River
See p76. 376 N. Michigan Ave.

Richard H. Driehaus Museum
See p77. 40 E. Erie St.

Swedish-American Museum and Children's Museum of Immigration
See pp101, 104. 5211 N. Clark St.

PARKS AND GARDENS

Urbs in Horto, City in a Garden, has long been Chicago's nickname, and you'll see why when you experience the city's parks and gardens—old, new and renewed. Park District gardeners plant over 550,000 annuals and perennials and 156,000 bulbs each year, along with 8,000 trees and shrubs. As a result, sweeping greens spaces, pocket parks, and even the medians and parkways of major thoroughfares such as Lake Shore Drive blossom with color.

Millennium Park★★★

Bounded by Michigan Ave., Randolph & Monroe Sts. and Columbus Dr. Open year-round daily 6am–11pm. 312-742-1168. www.millenniumpark.org.

Mayor Richard J. Daley's "park du triomphe" opened in the summer of 2004 to boisterous acclaim from critics and public alike. In spite of some grumbling about the gargantuan ($475 million!) price tag, most everyone agrees that the park is indeed a triumph. By day or night (it's beautifully illuminated in the evenings), this is no ordinary park. Though not one for pets (dogs are forbidden), the park's 24.5 acres beckon at every turn with something to see, touch or experience. Crowded with delights, Millennium Park offers an escape from the daily grind. And it serves another more practical purpose by masking an unsightly area of railroad tracks and parking lots that now operate below the park's well-manicured surface.

Best of the Millennium

Jay Pritzker Pavilion★★★ – Above all, literally, hovers the metallic mayhem of architect Frank Gehry's proscenium arch that marks this state-of-the-art outdoor theater. Sails, clouds, a cherry bomb in a soda can—everyone has an opinion about Gehry's oversized scramble of stainless steel, and you will too. The theater accommodates 4,000 in fixed seats and 7,000 on the oval-shaped fairway, which is covered with a trellis that holds speakers up and out of

BP Bridge, Millennium Park

Cloud Gate

Brook E. Collins/Chicago Park District

the way. This "waterproof" lawn is specially designed to drain away rainwater in 15 minutes. Gehry's 120-foot overhanging "headdress" shelters the stage itself, which is lined with pine wood. It's even air conditioned for the comfort of the **Grant Park Orchestra and Chorus** *(312-742-7638; www. grantparkmusicfesitval.com)*, which holds free concerts at the Pavilion throughout the summer.

Cloud Gate★★★ – Affectionately known as the Bean, this sculpture by Anish Kapoor has become the surprise favorite of the park. The gleaming structure of stainless steel—66 feet long, 33 feet high and weighing 110 tons—draws visitors like moths to a flame. Its jelly-bean shape creates fantastic reflections of the city skyline and the crowds—go ahead, walk up and pick yourself out. Better yet, step under the Bean and gaze up into its shiny underbelly. The effect is a kind of cross between a city gate, a majestic rotunda ceiling and a carnival mirror.

BP Bridge★★ – Getting there is all the fun on this meandering bridge designed by Frank Gehry. In 925

Crown Fountain

Brook E. Collins/Chicago Park District

feet of luxurious serpentine curves, the bridge connects Millennium and Grant parks over Columbus Drive. It's clad in stainless-steel panels that enclose walkers without the need for handrails. The broad hardwood deck slopes gently, inviting you to pause and take in the cityscape from every angle. Kids love to run the length of it (though this is frowned upon). The bridge also buffers the Pritzker Pavilion from traffic noise.

Crown Fountain★★ – For something completely different, check out the Crown Fountain, where huge projected faces spit water out of their mouths like modern gargoyles. The two 50-foot towers of steel, glass, light and water are the work of Spanish artist Jaume Plensa, and don't sound nearly as pleasing as they are in person. Best of all, a shallow, black-granite reflecting pool between the towers proves wonderful for wading and splashing as kids quickly discover. Watch carefully as the faces (a total of 300, soon to be 1,000), all Chicagoans, change slowly over the course of several minutes.

Lurie Garden★ – This planted sanctuary is truly a work in progress since the perennials will take a year or two to fill in and the protective pine hedgerow, known as the Shoulder Hedge, requires about ten years to mature. From the hedge, the garden slopes gently to the south to maximize its sun. A wooden boardwalk and watery pools, called the Seam, bisect the planted spaces.

Grant Park★★

Bounded by Roosevelt Rd. & Randolph St. on the north and south, and Michigan Ave. & Lake Shore Dr. on the west. 312-742-7648. www.chicagoparkdistrict.com.

Overshadowed by its glitzy neighbor Millennium Park, Grant Park remains dignified and beautiful in an old-fashioned way. The city's 319-acre "front yard" marks roughly the midpoint in the swath of parks that trims Chicago's 28-mile lakeshore. The park has been shaped by landfill, accretion, erosion and the human hand since 1830 when state commissioners set aside a thin strip of land along the shoreline to "remain forever open, clear

Brook E. Collins/Chicago Park District

Grant Park

63

Fests, Feasts and Fun in Grant Park

In the summer months, Grant Park is *the* place to be for Chicagoans and visitors. Topping the list of special events is **Taste of Chicago**, which attracts more than three million people over ten days to sample local eats (skip this festival on July 3 and 4 unless you enjoy a mob). No admission fee is charged, but food vendors only take tickets. Purchase tickets with cash or credit at any of several booths.

Grant Park also hosts Chicago's renowned music festivals, all held at the **Petrillo Bandshell** and featuring headline entertainment free of charge:

Chicago Blues Festival, 1st weekend in June

Chicago Gospel Festival, June

Chicago Country Music Festival, during the Taste of Chicago

Chicago Jazz Festival, Labor Day Weekend

and free." Sixty years later, mail-order magnate A. Montgomery Ward conducted a lengthy and successful battle with the city to clear the stables, railroad tracks and other eyesores that had rooted there in spite of the old edict.

In 1909 architect Daniel Burnham drew up a comprehensive plan for the city of Chicago calling for a "formal focal point," and the elegant landscaping of the park began to emerge as construction started in 1915. Though the automobile age sliced up the

green space with busy streets, the park still offers peaceful gardens, picnic spots and lovely vistas of the city and lake. Tennis courts and a playground occupy the park's shady northeast corner.

Fact: History was made in Grant Park on November 5, 2008, where Barack Obama was announced President Elect of America.

What's What in Grant Park

Museum Campus★★★ –
The southern part of the park is home to the city's popular triad of museums: **Field Museum of Natural History★★★**, **Shedd Aquarium★★★**, and **Adler Planetarium★★** *(see p51)*.

Buckingham Fountain★★
Columbus Dr. at Congress Pkwy.

Centerpiece of Grant Park, the Clarence Buckingham Memorial Fountain is truly a lakefront jewel. Donated to the city by philanthropist Kate Sturges Buckingham to honor her brother, the fountain was completed in 1927 at a cost of $750,000. A $2.8 million restoration completed in April 1995 returned the fountain to its

Buckingham Fountain

Brook E. Collins/Chicago Park District

MUST SEE

original splendor. It's modeled on a fountain at the Palace of Versailles in France, but is nearly twice as large. Intended to represent Lake Michigan, the fountain pumps 1.5 million gallons from the lake, recirculating all but what's lost through spray and evaporation—stand downwind on a hot, windy day for a refreshing spritz. Three basins of Georgia pink marble rise from the main pool; gargantuan carvings of seaweed and shells encircle the outside of each basin. In the large pool, four bronze sea horses, each 20 feet long, represent the states that border the lake.

If you become enamored of the Fountain (and really, who doesn't?) consider donating to the Parkways Foundation's $25 million restoration project. Some parts of the fountain have not been upgraded since 1927, and that many cold Chicago winters have wreaked havoc on the marble structure. *See www.restorethefountain.com for more information.*

A Fountain of Facts

- Buckingham Fountain is among the largest fountains in the world.
- At its maximum, the center jet shoots up 150 feet.
- The bottom pool measures 280 feet across, the lower basin is 103 feet, the middle basin is 60 feet and the upper basin is 24 feet.
- 820 lights color the fountain's water and light display.

Water and Light

As spectacular as the fountain's monumental scale are the water-and-light shows that flow from the basin during the summer. The fountain's 134 jets pump water at a rate of 14,100 gallons a minute and the central jet shoots water skyward to create a dazzling effect *(May–Oct dusk–11pm; 312-747-2474)*. Once controlled entirely by hand, the choreography of water and light is now regulated by computer.

Lincoln Park★★

Visitor Center: Lincoln Park Cultural Center, 2045 N. Lincoln Park West. 312-742-7726. www. chicagoparkdistrict.com. Open year-round Mon–Fri 9am–9pm, Sat 8am–4pm, Sun 10am–3pm.

Except for the occasional stray bone, it's hard to tell that this was once a soggy cemetery. Today the sweeping expanse is one of Chicago's most compelling landscapes. Unlike so many urban areas with waterfronts blighted by industry, Chicago provides unlimited access to the lake via its numerous lakefront parks. Among the finest is Lincoln Park.

The cemetery was established here in 1837, but as the city limits bulged northward from downtown, the cemetery's new neighbors lobbied for replacing it with parkland. Moving the corpses took time, but by the 1880s the

Touring Tip

To enjoy Lincoln Park start at the **Standing Lincoln** between LaSalle Street and North Avenue and wend your way north to Diversey Parkway.

Café Brauer

2021 N. Stockton Dr. Open year-round daily 11am–5pm. 312-742-2400.

This cafe makes a good stopping point on your walk through the park for a fresh brew or a bite to eat. In summer you can enjoy the beer garden overlooking South Pond. Architect Dwight Perkins, whose other credits include some of the animal houses at Lincoln Park Zoo, designed this refec-tory in 1908 for restaurateurs Paul and Caspar Brauer. A striking example of the Prairie school style, it hugs the pond with its main pavilion and flanking loggias. Arts and Crafts details—chandeliers, tiles, mosaics and windows—lend the interior a suitably rustic charm.

heart of the park was well estab-lished. Filling in the land over the next decades extended the park to its northern limits by 1957. Today stretching six miles and 1,200 acres along the shoreline of Lake Michigan, from Oak Street north to Ardmore Avenue, Lincoln Park trims the city's watery edge with a pleasant and peaceful greenbelt.

At North Avenue, the park forms the northern edge of the affluent **Gold Coast★** *(see p32)*, and at Clark Street, the eastern boundary of the lively **Lincoln Park/ DePaul★** neighborhood, where theaters, restaurants and shops abound.

Alfred Caldwell Lilly Pool

Brook E. Collins/Chicago Park District

A Walk in the Park

Lincoln Park Zoo★★ – *See p99.* 2200 N. Cannon Dr.

Peggy Notebaert Nature Museum★ – *See p59.* 2430 N. Cannon Dr.

Alfred Caldwell Lily Pool★ – *Enter from the north off Fullerton Pkwy.*

Lincoln Park

Brook E. Collins/Chicago Park District

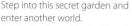

All That Glitters

Wondering what that glittery gold structure located south of the conservatory beyond the elevated tracks is? Known as the "Gold Dome Building" *(100 N. Central Park Ave.)* for obvious reasons, it was built in 1928 as the headquarters of the West Park Commission. The structure serves today as Garfield Park's fieldhouse. Its sparkling gold dome now looks out of place in the gritty neighborhood that surrounds the park, but in its heyday the building was no doubt an elegant addition to the banks of the park's original lagoon.

Step into this secret garden and enter another world.

Originally planned in the Victorian style in the 1880s, the garden was reshaped as a wooded grove in 1937 by landscape architect Alfred Caldwell.

The plot spent much of its life as the zoo's Rookery until Caldwell's Prairie-style vision was restored in 2002. Today this tranquil enclave is a haven for birds and birdwatchers alike.

Lincoln Park Conservatory –
2391 N. Stockton Dr.
312-742-7736. Open year-round
daily 9am–5pm.

Modeled in 1892 on London's Crystal Palace, the glass and copper structure and its 15 propagating houses, greenhouses and gardens now cover three acres.

Garfield Park Conservatory★

300 N. Central Park Ave., in Garfield Park. 312-746-5100. www.garfield conservatory.org. Open year-round daily 9am–5pm, Thu 9am–8pm.

Built in 1908 by landscape architect Jens Jensen, Garfield Park

Brook E. Collins/Chicago Park District

Garfield Park Conservatory

World's Columbian Exposition

In a battle to host the 1893 World's Columbian Exposition, Chicago earned its enduring nickname "Windy City" because of all the blustery boasting that led to its winning the honor over other cities. Conceived to celebrate the 400th anniversary of Columbus' discovery of America, this world fair covered 650 acres along present-day Jackson Park and encompassed 200 buildings erected by leading architects. From opening day on May 1, 1893 through October, the exposition awed 27 million visitors with its architecture and attractions, including the world's first Ferris wheel and the infamous "Little Egypt" dancing the hootchie kootchie. Floodlights illuminated the Neoclassical buildings, creating a sparkling white, fairylike atmosphere. But the fair was fleeting as its construction was done entirely of "staff," a temporary material left to crumble away at the event's end.

Conservatory has become popular for exhibits that integrate sculpture or objects (such as dinosaur skeletons) into the foliage. Look for the work that glass artist **Dale Chihuly** left in the Aroid House after his big show here in 2001. The conservatory mounts several shows a year, as well as market days on summer weekends. Restoration of the conservatory has created stunning results; the newly renovated **Palm House**, for example, contains 3,500 plants.

Jackson Park

E. 56th to 57th Sts., Stony Island Ave. to Lake Michigan. www.chicagoparkdistrict.com.

Located eight miles south of the Loop along Lake Michigan's shoreline, the park's 600 acres of playing fields, lagoons and lush vegetation began as a wasteland of sand dunes and scrub marshes. Famed landscape architect Frederick Law Olmsted (designer of Central Park in New York City) first laid out the park in 1870. He later redesigned and completed it for the World's Columbian Exposition in 1893, creating a series of lagoons and

Jackson Park

Brook E. Collins/Chicago Park District

formal ponds as its centerpiece. In addition to the features that remain from the fair, Jackson Park features an 18-hole golf course. Fragments of the fair include **Columbia Basin★**, a reflecting pool designed by Olmsted for the Palace of Fine Arts, now the **Museum of Science and Industry★★★**; **Osaka Gardens★**, at the north end of the sanctuary on Wooded Island; and **The Republic★**, the 24-foot-high "Golden Lady" cast by Daniel Chester French—the only sculpture in the park.

Osaka Gardens, Jackson Park

Brook E. Collins/Chicago Park District

GREATER CHICAGO

0   3mi
0   6km

GLENCOE, LAKE FOREST \ Chicago Botanic Garden★★

WILMETTE
★★NORTH SHORE
★Baha'i House of Worship★★
SKOKIE
Northwestern University
EVANSTON
Rogers Park
★Lifeline Theatre

LAKE MICHIGAN

O'HARE AIRPORT
Rosehill Cemetery
★Puppet Parlor
UPTOWN ★Wilson Skatepark
Graceland Cemetery★★
Lincoln Park★★
★**LINCOLN PARK/ DEPAUL**
Marovitz
★Wrigley Field
★Bailiwick Rep. Theater
Athenaeum Theatre
★Peggy Notebaert Nature Museum
★Apollo Theater
★**MAGNIFICENT MILE**
★★★
Humboldt Park
★Vittum Theater
United Center
★★★**THE LOOP**
★Garfield Park Conservatory
★★★OAK PARK
Garfield Park
NEAR WEST SIDE
★Mexican Fine Arts Center Museum■
CHINATOWN
BRIDGEPORT CANARYVILLE
PILSEN
U.S. Cellular Field
★Burnham Skatepark
Burnham Park
BRONZEVILLE
NEAR SOUTH SIDE
★★Robie House
HYDE PARK KENWOOD
★David and Alfred Smart Museum of Art
★★★**MUSEUM OF SCIENCE AND INDUSTRY**
Washington Park
DuSable Museum of African-American History
Jackson Park
★63rd St. Beach
★★**UNIVERSITY OF CHICAGO**
Oriental Institute★★
South Shore
Oak Woods Cemetery
ILLINOIS INDIANA

MIDWAY AIRPORT

★Brookfield Zoo | Morton Arboretum★
★Illinois & Michigan Canal NHS |

★**PULLMAN HISTORIC DISTRICT**

Hotels
1. City Suites Hotel
2. Hawthorne Terrace
3. The Homestead
4. Hotel Orrington
5. Majestic Hotel
6. The Willows Hotel
7. Wooded Isle Suites

Restaurants
1. Andies
2. Ann Sather
3. Aruns
4. Club Lucky
5. Davis Street Fishmarket
6. Erwin
7. Green Zebra
8. Half Shell
9. Healthy Food
10. Heaven on Seven
11. Hema's Kitchen
12. Pasteur
13. Tapas Barcelona
● Trio Atelier

PARKS AND GARDENS

HISTORIC SITES

Chicago's fascinating history takes in industry and robber barons, immigrants and labor movements, and, of course, architecture. Here are some of our favorite sites from the city's past.

Graceland Cemetery

Anne Culberson/Michelin

movers and shakers. Developed in 1860, Graceland received many of the corpses that were exhumed from the lakeshore cemetery where construction of Lincoln Park was underway. Stroll the 119-acre grounds yourself (pick up a site plan at the entrance) or check with the Chicago Architecture Foundation about its next Graceland tour. And no, Elvis is not buried here.

Graceland Cemetery★★

4001 N. Clark St., Lakeview. From downtown, take Lake Shore Dr. north and turn left on Irving Park Rd. to the cemetery. 773-525-1105. www.graceland cemetery.org. Open year-round daily 8am–4:30pm. Closed Dec 25, July 4 & Labor Day.

For a slice of Chicago history, check out this cemetery, just north of Wrigley Field, where notable architecture and sculpture mark the resting places of many of the city's

Notable Residents

Be sure to pay a visit to the tombs of Henry Harrison Getty and Martin Ryerson (both designed by Louis Sullivan), Marshall Field (designed by Daniel Chester French), Potter and Bertha Palmer, Daniel Burnham, Peter Schoenhofen and George Pullman *(see p74)*, all in the northern half of the cemetery. To the south rest boxing great Jack Johnson and National League founder William Hulbert, who is spending eternity under a large baseball.

More Local Haunts

If Graceland shelters the remains of Chicago's historic elite, the lovely **Rosehill** *(5800 N. Ravenswood Ave.; 773-561-5940)* hosts local merchants, bankers and businessmen who made this the City that Works. Many of Chicago's mayors rest here, along with Civil War generals and soldiers. Founded in 1859, Rosehill is Chicago's largest cemetery. If the Gothic entryway looks familiar, it's because it replicates the **Water Tower and Pumping Station★** downtown *(see p42)*.
On the city's South Side, **Oak Woods Cemetery** *(1035 E. 67th St.; 773-288-3800)* is even older (1854), and lodges some of the city's most interesting residents: Mayor Harold Washington, Chicago's first African-American mayor; Olympian Jesse Owens; activist Ida B. Wells; and physicist Enrico Fermi. *For more about local cemeteries, visit www.graveyards.com.*

MUST SEE

Can't Get Enough Frank Lloyd Wright?

Calling all FLW fans. You've been to Robie House *(see below)*. You've been to Oak Park *(see p78)*. But wait, there's more. A handful of Wright's residential architecture (all privately owned) still stands in Chicago, much of it on the South Side:

Adams House (1900-01)	9326 S. Pleasant Ave.
American System-Built Houses (1917)	10410 and 10541 S. Hoyne Ave.
Bach House (1915)	7415 N. Sheridan Rd.
Foster House and Stable (1900)	12147 S. Harvard Ave.
Heller House (1897)	5132 S. Woodlawn Ave.
Roloson Houses (1894)	3213–19 S. Calumet Ave.
Waller Apartments (1895)	2840–48 W. Walnut St.
Walser House (1903)	42 N. Central Ave.

Robie House★★

5757 S. Woodlawn Ave., on the University of Chicago campus. Take Lake Shore Dr. south to 53rd St. and turn left on Woodlawn Ave. 708-848-1976. www.gowright.org. Visit by one-hour guided tour only, year-round Mon–Fri 11am, 1pm & 3pm, weekends every 20min 11am–3:30pm. Closed Jan 1, Thanksgiving Day & Dec 25. $9. By bus, take #6 Jackson Park Express to Stony Island Ave. & 57th St.; walk west 6 blocks to Woodlawn Ave. and go left one block.

This home made its designer, **Frank Lloyd Wright**, world famous and helped "break the box" of traditional architecture. In 1908, wealthy inventor Frederick Robie commissioned architect Wright to design his residence in Hyde Park. The resulting home, with its distinctive horizontal lines, is considered a masterpiece of modern architecture.

The Robies lived here only for a year or so, after which time the house passed through a number of different owners. It was saved from the wrecking ball at the 11th hour in 1957 and is now operated by the University of Chicago in conjunction with the Frank Lloyd Wright Home and Studio Foundation, which is supervising an intensive ten-year restoration.

©University of Chicago/Peter Kiar

Robie House

Inside, the hallmarks of the Prairie style are all here: the long, low horizontal lines, side-hinging casement windows, the hidden front entrance, built-in furniture and the grand hearth that separates living from dining space. Stained, leaded and art-glass windows are done in geometric patterns, and Wright's trademark globe-shaped "moonlight" ceiling fixtures provide lighting. Note the long Roman bricks that Wright favored, which accentuate the horizontal even more.

Hutchinson Street District★

Between Lake Shore Dr & Hazel St. www.cityofchicago.org/Land marks/H/HutchinsonStreet.html.

Several designs by Prairie School architect George Washington Maher, together with a range of eclectic, single-family homes, provide a welcome diversion from the high-rise lakefront landscape in the Lakeview neighborhood. The **Edwin J. Mosser House** (1902) at no. 750, features oversized urns and a Sullivan-esque entrance facing Clarendon Street. At no. 817, the two-story **Claude Seymour House** (1913) is

distinguished by banded leaded-glass windows, urns and a wide, overhanging roofline and Maher's signature flattened-arch entrance. Maher's **Grace Brackenbush House** (no. 839) marks the integration of picturesque period revival elements with the horizontal emphasis of the Prairie school. The 1894 **John C. Scales House** (no. 840) resembles a Queen Anne home replete with shingles and round turrets.

Jane Addams Hull-House Museum★

800 S. Halsted St., on the University of Illinois campus. From the Loop, drive west on W. Adams St. and turn south on Halsted St. 312-413-5353. www.uic.edu/jaddams/hull. Open Tue–Fri 10am–4pm, Sun noon–4pm. Closed major holidays.

If you're interested in the history of immigration in Chicago, Hull House is for you. Founded in 1889 by pioneering social workers Jane Addams and Ellen Gates Starr, the settlement house became a focal point for citywide and national movements to improve living and working conditions of the nation's poor and disadvantaged. Observing similar work in London

MUST SEE

Jane Addams Hull-House Museum

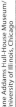
Jane Addams Hull-House Museum/
University of Illinois, Chicago

(England) in 1886, 26-year-old Addams returned to Chicago inspired. In 1889 she and Starr moved into a Near West Side neighborhood teeming with immigrant families (the house they occupied was built in 1856 by real-estate developer Charles Hull). Through their dedication to helping the poor, and their aggressive agenda of education, social service and reform, Hull-House grew to a complex of 13 buildings—including Chicago's first public gymnasium, art and music schools and a cooperative residence for working women. Today only the house and the Residents' Dining Hall remain, renovated and converted into a museum. The house itself is furnished in the Victorian style with many original pieces, including Jane Addams' desk.

Prairie Avenue Historic District★

Drive south from the Loop on Michigan Ave., turn left at 18th St. and continue two blocks to Prairie Ave. (no through traffic). www.cityofchicago.org/Landmarks/P/PrairieAveDistrict.html.

The area south of downtown ranks today among the hippest, fastest-growing residential section of the city. Though it seems like a modern phenomenon, it all started along Prairie Avenue after the Chicago Fire in 1871. Here on

While You're in the Neighborhood . . .

Around the corner from Glessner House, the **National Vietnam Veterans Art Museum** exhibits a powerful collection of works by veterans of the war in Southeast Asia *(1801 S. Indiana Ave.; 312-326-0270; www.nvvam.org; not recommended for children)*. Once the Chess Records Studio, famous for recording Muddy Waters, Howlin' Wolf, Chuck Berry and other blues greats, **Blues Heaven** *(2120 S. Michigan Ave; 312-808-1286; www.bluesheaven.com)* now houses a foundation created to document the blues and to support blues artists *(studio tours Mon–Fri noon–3pm, Sat noon–2pm)*.

"Millionaire's Row" lived industrial and commercial leaders Marshall Field and George Pullman, among others, in mansions designed by famous architects such as Richard Morris Hunt, Burnham & Root, and Henry Hobson Richardson. For a while, Prairie Avenue was the city's most fashionable address, but families moved to the North Side as industry invaded the neighborhood after 1900. In contrast, State Street between 16th and 22nd streets became the notorious Levee, an area of saloons and brothels. By 1966 industrial growth had caused the demolition of most of Prairie Avenue's mansions; a Chicago Landmark District was created in 1979 to preserve the remaining homes.

House Museums

Two of the city's most historically significant house museums form the district's core. One-hour tours of either or both *(312-326-1480)* begin at the coach house of Glessner House. Neighborhood tours are offered on alternating Sundays from July to September.

John Jacob Glessner House★★
1800 S. Prairie Ave. www.glessner house.org. Tours Wed–Sun 1pm & 3pm. Closed major holidays.

Designed by H.H. Richardson in 1886, the Glessner House revolutionized domestic American architecture with its open floor plan and plain facade. John Glessner, a manufacturer of farm implements, commissioned the house at a time when labor unrest alarmed the city's wealthy residents.
In response, the architect designed the mansion like a fortress by turning its back to the street and including a secure inner courtyard.

Henry B. Clarke House★
1855 S. Indiana Ave. 312/326-1480. www.clarkhousemuseum.org. Tours Wed–Sun noon & 2pm. Closed major holidays.

Built in 1836 for New York merchant Henry Clarke in the Greek Revival style (notice the heavy columns on the front porch), this white clapboard home is considered Chicago's oldest structure. It was moved here in 1977 from South Wabash Avenue.

Pullman Historic District★

Between 107th & 115th Sts. along Cottage Grove Ave. 773-785-8901. www.pullmanil.org.

Located in an industrial district on the Far South Side, this fascinating community was created by railroad-car magnate **George Pullman**—famous for his luxurious train coaches—in 1881 as an experimental company town. He incorporated the Pullman Palace Car Company in 1867, but ten years later striking rail workers shocked the nation and open conflict between labor and management threatened. Wishing to isolate his employees from

Glessner House Museum

Glessner House Museum/Hedrich Blessing

the strike- and strife-prone city, Pullman built his new factory town on 500 acres 13 miles south of Chicago. He hired architect Solon Beman and landscaper Nathan F. Barrett to design the factories and a comprehensive town plan. Pullman ran his "perfect town" for a profit, collecting rents from workers and providing services and necessities. Ever the capitalist, Pullman maintained ownership of all the property in his community; he set rents and refused to let anyone own individual houses. But economic depression in the 1890s brought wage cuts, and to keep the town profitable, Pullman raised rents and food prices. The company's employees rebelled, and strikes and bloody conflict led to the end of Pullman's plan. In 1971 the town was listed on the National Register of Historic Places; its restoration continues today.

A Walk Through the District

After years of neglect, the community was lovingly restored and today is best sampled by a stroll down the 19th century streets. A variety of Victorian residences fill the 16 blocks of the South Pullman residential district. The larger homes of managers face 111th Street, while smaller row houses and double houses of craftsmen and workers line the streets south to 115th Street. Varied and picturesque rooflines are typical of

Historic Pullman Foundation

Houses in Pullman Historic District

HISTORIC SITES

75

Hotel Florence

Historic Pullman Foundation

the Queen Anne style so popular among Victorian architects (but more often seen on larger houses). Architect Solon Beman also designed the simpler homes of North Pullman *(between 104th & 108th Sts.)* for workers of two other factories; the most charming stretch runs along Cottage Grove Avenue at 107th Street, where the houses are staggered along the angling thoroughfares. Most homes are private residences, so you will be looking at exteriors only, but a number of historic homes are open for viewing the second weekend in October for the Annual Pullman House Tour *(11am–5pm; $18 at the door, $15 in advance)*. On the tour, you'll see a cross-section of private Pullman residences, from ornate mansions to simple workers' cottages and multi-unit apartments..

Though it's closed for restoration, you can still see the exterior of the **Hotel Florence** *(1111 S. Forestville Ave.)*—named for Pullman's daughter—which was off-limits to workers and where only visiting businessmen could drink.

Rest in Peace

Pullman's social experiment did not end well, and employees turned on him in anger when he lowered wages but refused to lower rents. When he died in 1897, his family was so worried that his grave in Graceland Cemetery would be robbed that they covered the coffin in tar paper and asphalt, sealing it into a concrete block. Railroad ties were used to overlay and safeguard the tomb further. As far as we know, the sleeping-car prince still rests securely in peace.

McCormick Tribune Bridgehouse and Chicago River Museum

376 N. Michigan Ave. 312-977-0227. www.bridgehousemuseum. org. Open May–Oct, Thu–Mon 10am–5pm and during select bridge lifts. Admission to the museum is $3 adults. Free for kids. www.pullmanil.org.

It had been almost 40 years since this bridge tower, the southwest tower of the Michigan Avenue Bridge, was used for bridge tenders. While it may have looked striking on the outside, it was all but forgotten on the inside. The non-profit Friends of the Chicago River raised funds to lease the historic space from the city of Chicago, and turned it into a museum that illustrated how the city grew up on the river. Exhibits include information on the river and ecology, the role the river played in the city's founding and the city's many bridges. Check the schedule to try to visit during one of the 100 times annually when the bridge is lifted to accommodate sailboats. It is a feat of engineering.

The exterior of the tower, which is visible even when the museum is not open, features bas reliefs of important moments in the city's history, including the Great Chicago Fire. The reliefs were sculpted by J.E. Fraser and Henry Hering in 1928.

Richard H. Driehaus Museum

40 E. Erie St. 312-932-8665. www.driehausmuseum.org. $25 adults, $15 children ages 12–16. Children under the age of 12 are not permitted in the museum.

Nestled in the recently renovated former mansion of Samuel M. Nickerson is the city's newest museum. Built between 1879 and 1883, Nickerson's Marble Palace was one of the prime examples of the Gilded Age in Chicago, built in a Richardsonian Romanesque

style and possibly one of the most expensive homes ever built in Chicago. Richard H. Driehaus, a well-known Chicago businessman, bought the mansion in 2003 and spent five years bringing it back to its Marble Palace-era glory—part of his ongoing attempt to get Chicagoans to appreciate and protect Neoclassicism as much as they do modern architecture. Along with original furnishings, the mansion now houses Driehaus' collection of fine and decorative arts, including Tiffany lamps and windows, and other opulent decorative items of eras gone by. When it first opened the museum was only available for tours by appointment, with plans to add regular operating hours later.

Stephen A. Douglas Tomb and Memorial

636 E. 35th St. 312-225-2620. www.illinoishistory.gov/hs/doug las_tomb.htm. Wed–Sun, call for hours. Free.

U. S. Sen. Stephen A. Douglas (1813–1861) is best known for his performance in his debates against Abraham Lincoln. His gravesite sports a 96-foot-tall tower, the top of which can be seen from Lake Shore Drive. Most locals just drive past, but exiting the Drive is worthwhile. The mausoleum contains four bronze allegorical figures representing Illinois, history, justice and eloquence. In addition to the tomb, the Bronzeville site has well-manicured gardens and grass, providing a surprising serene state park nestled in a busy, urban neighborhood.

EXCURSIONS

Need a break from bustling downtown? A jaunt beyond the city limits reveals different worlds in any direction. Beaches and dunes lie south and east, history to the southwest, beautiful trees and great architecture to the west, and lovely gardens to the north. So take your pick!

Frank Lloyd Wright Home and Studio

©Courtesy of Frank Lloyd Wright Preservation Trust/Photo Don Kalec

Oak Park★★★

10mi west of Chicago via I-290 West to Harlem Ave. exit. Turn right on Harlem Ave. and proceed north. Visitor information: 708-524-7800 or 888-625-7275; www.visitoak park.com. See map p81.

What do the modern house, *For Whom the Bell Tolls* and Tarzan have in common? Oak Park, of course! Perhaps best known for its enclave of homes designed by architect **Frank Lloyd Wright** *(see box, p79)*, Oak Park is also the birthplace of Ernest Hemingway and the one-time home of Edgar Rice Burroughs, creator of Tarzan. Founded after the Great Chicago Fire in 1871 by a prosperous Puritan population, the little suburb grew rapidly. Today Oak Park is economically stable and socially progressive, accommodating various lifestyles with relative ease. Its shady, tree-lined streets, historic

Touring Tip: Visiting Oak Park

If you arrive by car, the Lake Street parking garage *(between Kenilworth & Forest Aves.)* is most central to the attractions. To get there by public transportation, take the CTA Green or Blue Line, or take the Metra West commuter rail from the Metra station at W. Madison and Canal Sts. Exit all train lines at Oak Park Ave. or Harlem Ave. *(312-836-7000. www.metrarail.com)*. You can catch the Oak Park Shuttle at train stations around town *(daily 10am–5:30pm; 708-343-4830)*.

The Oak Park Visitors Center *(158 N. Forest Ave.; 888-625-7275; www.visitoak park.com; open year-round daily 10am–5pm; closed Jan 1, Thanksgiving Day & Dec 25)* is a good place to pick up maps and guides, buy attraction tickets, and rent a guided audio tour for your walk around the neighborhood *($10)*.

Frank Lloyd Wright

Frank Lloyd Wright's best-known works revolutionized residential building design. Born in Wisconsin in 1867, Wright came early under the influence of renowned architect Louis Sullivan, apprenticing in Sullivan's studio until striking out on his own at age 25. Living and working in Oak Park, he developed his distinctive Prairie style, its strong horizontal lines and overhanging eaves inspired by the flat midwestern landscape. Inside, Wright flowed rooms one into another and he designed furniture to complement his organic designs. In a scandal that effectively ended his practice in socially conservative Oak Park, Wright left his wife and six children in 1909. Wright remained in the limelight until his death in 1959 at age 91. His total number of designs exceeds 1,100, nearly half of which were actually built.

attractions, upscale boutiques and cozy restaurants make the suburb a must-see destination, especially for architecture buffs.

Frank Lloyd Wright Home and Studio★★

951 Chicago Ave. 708-848-1976. www.wrightplus.org. Visit by 45min guided tours only, year-round Mon–Fri 11am, 1pm & 3pm; weekends 11am–3:30pm. Closed Jan 1, Thanksgiving Day & Dec 25. $12.

Wright first built this house in 1889 and continued to remodel and add to it over time; his alterations reveal his architectural growth. Restored to its 1909 appearance, when Wright last lived there, the original structure features the horizontal bands of windows and low profile of the Prairie style. Notice the cozy inglenook in the living room and the signature furnishings, all designed by Wright.

Unity Temple★★

875 W. Lake St. 708-383-8873. www.unitytemple-utrf.org. Open Dec–Feb daily 1pm–4pm. Rest of the year Mon–Fri 10:30am– 4:30pm, weekends 1pm–4pm.

Guided tours weekends 1pm, 2pm & 3pm. Pre-arranged, customized tours are available by calling 708-383-8873 Closed Jan 1, Thanksgiving Day & Dec 25.

Wright called this Unitarian temple "my jewel," and it's easy to see why. This, the last of his major public buildings still standing, celebrated its centenary in 2008.

Forest Avenue★

Walk south from Wright's home and studio to see a wonderful cross-section of his residential work (pick up information at the visitor center).

Begin by wandering west on Chicago Avenue. Numbers 1019, 1027 and 1031 are "bootleg" homes that the 25-year-old architect designed in violation of his exclusive contract with Adler & Sullivan in 1892–93.

The 1902 **Frank W. Thomas House★** at no. 10 is considered Wright's first true Prairie-style house; it abandons all the fuss of Victorian design that you see in the row houses just south.

EXCURSIONS

The Rest of Oak Park's Best

"Pleasant Home"★

217 S. Home Ave. 708-383-2654. www.oprf.com/phf. Visit by one-hour guided tour only, Mar–Nov 12:30pm, 1:30pm & 2:30pm. Rest of the year Thu–Sun 12:30pm & 1:30pm. Closed major holidays. $5.

"Pleasant Home"

Oak Park Area Convention and Visitors Bureau

Here's a Prairie-style home designed by another architect, George Washington Maher (1864–1926), whose work can be seen throughout the suburbs of Chicago. He designed the 30-room "Pleasant Home" (aka Farson-Mills House) in 1897 for banker John Farson.

Ernest Hemingway Birthplace

339 N. Oak Park Ave. 708-848-2222. www.hemingway.org. Visit by guided tour only, year-round Sun–Fri 1pm–5pm, Sat 10am–5pm. $8.

This restored Victorian home built in 1890 re-creates the comfortable family upbringing of celebrated author Ernest Hemingway (1899–1961). A visit here also provides a glimpse of Oak Park's social order in the early 20th century and the impact that the community had on the author's early development. Two blocks south, the Hemingway Museum *(200 N. Oak Park Ave.; same hours & contact information as Birthplace; $7)* focuses on the first 20 years of the writer's life.

North Shore★★

31mi from downtown Chicago to Lake Forest. Follow Lake Shore Dr. /Sheridan Rd. north.

Chicago's northern suburbs collectively conjure up a vision of elegant living called the North Shore. The lovely—and unusual—geography of ravines, bluffs, beaches and woodlands,

North Shore

Northshore Convention and Visitors Bureau

Map legend:

Hotels
- 🏨 The Carleton of Oak Park
- 🏨 The Write Inn

Restaurants
- ① Avenue Ale House
- ② Café le Coq

and the area's architecture and history combine to make a drive up the shore an enjoyable one-day excursion. Take your time and stop for lunch, take a peek around a village center, or a enjoy one of the many beaches along the way. (During summer, some townships charge nonresidents for beach or park admission.)

Brookfield Zoo★★
See p97. 8400 W. 31st St.

Getting To Know the North Shore

Bahá'í House of Worship★★

100 Linden Ave., Wilmette. 847-853-2300. www.us.bahai. org/how. Open year-round daily 7am–6:30pm; visitor center open year-round daily 10am–5pm. Guided tours Sun 1:45pm.

The lacy, opalescent dome of the Baha'i temple will startle you as you cross from Evanston to Wilmette on Sheridan Road. The

mammoth, nine-sided structure, rising 191 feet, cuts an exotic profile against the low suburban skyline. This is the North American seat of the Baha'i faith, whose members follow the teachings of the 19th century Persian prophet Baha'u'llah, believing in the "oneness" of religion and of humankind. Why is the only North American temple located here? The religion was introduced at the 1893 World's Columbian Exposition held in Chicago. Construction of the temple, which began in 1909, took nearly 50 years to complete.

Chicago Botanic Garden★★

1000 Lake Cook Rd., Glencoe. 25mi north of Chicago via I-90/94 West to I-94 and US-41. Exit at Lake Cook Rd. and go east .5mi. 847-835-5440. www.chicago-botanic.org. Open year-round daily 8am–dusk. Closed Dec 25. Parking $15/car.

With 26 garden areas, more than a million individual plants of 7,000

EXCURSIONS

81

Downtown Evanston and Central Street a little farther north both teem with restaurants and shops. In Wilmette, try **Convito Italiano** *(1515 Sheridan Rd., in Plaza del Lago; 847-251-0123; www.convitoitaliano.com)* for a delightful trattoria lunch or dinner, or the makings of a gourmet picnic from its market.

Tiny **Ravinia Bistro** *(581 Roger Williams Ave., Highland Park; 847-432-1033)* serves French country fare and delectable pastries. Along Sheridan Road in Highwood, you'll find a gaggle of notable French and Italian restaurants. When you reach Lake Forest, stop by **Market Square★** *(700 N. Western Ave.)*, a village shopping and dining center since the early 1900s.

different varieties and a host of bird life, the 385-acre preserve makes a lovely stop at any time of year. The heart of the garden occupies the largest of nine islands in a 60-acre artificial lagoon.

Begin at the **Gateway Visitor Center**, and consider a tram tour *(late Apr–Oct daily 10am–3:30pm; $5)* for a narrated overview. Highlights include the formal **Rose Garden★**, the six "rooms" of the **English Walled Garden★**, the tactile and fragrant **Sensory Garden**, and the **Japanese Garden★**, called Sansho-En ("the garden of three islands"). In summer, kids will enjoy the **Model Railroad Garden**, 7,500 square feet of miniature American landscapes crisscrossed by 15 model train lines *(open daily 10am–5pm; $3)*. You can have a sit-down

Chicago Botanic Garden

Chicago Botanic Garden

lunch or a snack here, too, in the **Garden Café**, the outdoor **Grille**, or the **Rose Terrace Café**.

Morton Arboretum★

4100 Rte. 53, Lisle. 25mi west of downtown via I-290 West to I-88 tollway West; exit on Rte. 53 and go north. 630-968-0074. www.morton arb.org. Open Apr–Oct daily 7am–7pm (or sunset, depending which is earlier). Rest of the year daily 7am–5pm. Gatehouse fees: $9, $6 children (3–17).

Joy Morton used the fortune he made at the helm of Morton Salt Company to establish this arboretum on 400 acres in 1922. Today sprawling over 1,700 acres, the outdoor museum is both a serious scientific laboratory of woody plants from around the world and a lovely place to spend the day. You'll find oaks, elms, lindens, sugar maples and 3,300 other tree and plant types organized into family groups, landscape groups, geographic groups and habitat groups. Whether you choose to hike the 14 miles of trails, drive the nine-mile circuit or spend the day exploring the 36,000-square-foot **visitor center** and surrounding gardens, you're in for a treat. There is also a Children's Garden to keep

MUST SEE

the little ones amused *(Apr–Oct 9:30am–5pm, Nov–Feb 9:30am–4pm, until 6:30pm Thu May–Sept).*

Mitchell Museum of the American Indian
See p57. 3001 Central St., Evanston.

Illinois & Michigan Canal National Heritage Corridor★

Southwest of Chicago via I-55 South to Rtes. 45 & 171. Visitor information: Heritage Corridor Convention and Visitors Bureau, 800-926-2262 or www.heritage corridorcvb.com; and the Canal Corridor Association, 815-588-1100 or www.canalcor.org.

Running 96 miles from Bridge-port to LaSalle/Peru, the Illinois & Michigan (I&M) Canal first linked the Great Lakes to the Mississippi in 1848 and helped Chicago build its reputation as an industrial powerhouse. Until 1882 when steamboats took over, mules pulled barges laden with lumber, stone and grains through 15 locks that equalized the 160-foot differ-ence in water level between the canal in Chicago and the Illinois River. By 1914, the new Sanitary and Ship Canal replaced the north-ern section, and in 1933 the Illinois River was made navigable in the southern reaches.
Now long obsolete, the canal is preserved in a **National Heritage Corridor** and a series of parks, trails and preserves. The waterway

Best Ways to Experience the National Heritage Corridor
The scenic 61-mile **I&M Canal State Trail★** runs along the old towpath from Rockdale to LaSalle *(access at Channahon, Exit 248 from I-55)* and provides a historic route you can hike, bike or snow-mobile. At LaSalle, where the canal and Heritage Corridor end, you'll find **Lock no. 14★**, the only lock that is completely restored *(Canal Rd., off Rte. 351).*

passes through suburbs and industrial areas, as well as the historic canal towns of **Lemont**, **Lockport★**, **Joliet★**, **Morris**, **Seneca**, **Marseilles**, **Ottawa★**, **Utica** and **LaSalle**, some more ravaged than burnished by time.

Lockport★

15mi southwest of Chicago via I-55 South to LaGrange Rd./Rte. 45 (Exit 279A).

As the location of Lock no. 1 and the old Canal Commission head-quarters, Lockport once bustled with the comings and goings of barges, canallers, merchants, wagons and mules. Old grain warehouses—the Gaylord and the Norton buildings—bookend the historic district, which encom-passes the blocks between the canal and 7th, Washington and 11th streets. Restored to its 1860s appearance, the **Gaylord Build-ing★** *(200 W. 8th St.; 815-588-1100;*

Touring Tip
During good weather, enjoy the full sweep of the arboretum on the **Acorn Express**, a narrated, one-hour, open-air tram tour *(departs from the visitor center year-round; 630-968-0074; $5).*

EXCURSIONS

Fine Dining on the Prairie

One of the region's finest restaurants occupies a restored 1895 building in Lockport's historic district. **Tallgrass** *(1006 S. State St.; 815-838-5566)* offers contemporary French cuisine in prix-fixe menus of three, four or five courses. For lunch, or a less pricey dinner, choose **Public Landing** *(815-838-6500)*, located in the Gaylord Building. Farther down the pike, enjoy lunch or dinner in the rustic supper-club atmosphere at **Starved Rock Lodge** *(Rtes. 178 & 71; 800-868-7625; www.starvedrocklodge.com)*.

Lockport

Anne Culberson/Michelin

www.canalcor.org/gaylord; open year-round Tue–Sat 11am–6pm, Sun noon–5pm) features an information desk and exhibits that explore the history of the canal and its impact on Illinois. To the south, the 1850 **Norton Building** now houses the **Lockport Gallery**, which exhibits the work of past and present Illinois artists *(201 W. 10th St.; 815-838-7400; www. museum.state.il.us/ismsites/lock*

port/; open year-round Mon–Fri 9am–5pm, Sun noon–5pm; closed major holidays). In between the Gaylord and Norton buildings, the **Pioneer Settlement★** *(815-838-0549; open May–Sept daily 1pm–4:30pm)* of 19th century buildings spreads for a block along the canal's edge. The **I&M Canal Museum** is located in the original Canal Commission headquarters *(803 South State St.; 815-838-5080; visit by guided tour only, year-round daily 1pm–4:30pm)*. Walk the 2.5-mile **Gaylord Donnelley Canal Trail★** for a look at the massive limestone walls of Lock no. 1. West of the canal extends the lovely, 269-acre **Lockport Prairie Nature Preserve★** *(Rte. 53 & Division St.; 815-727-8700; www.fpdwc.org/lock port.cfm; open Apr–Oct daily 8am–8pm; rest of the year daily 8am–5pm)*.

Gaylord Building

Anne Culberson/Michelin

Reddick Mansion

Anne Culberson/Michelin

Ottawa★

79mi southwest of Chicago via I-55 South to Rte. 23 (Exit 90).

This town was built on glass. Silica sand from its famous quarries was shipped to and fro on the canal, and by 1900, the city was a leading glass producer.

In **Washington Park**, senatorial candidates Abraham Lincoln and Stephen A. Douglas held the first of their famous 1858 debates. Douglas was a frequent guest at the 1856 **Reddick Mansion★**, adjacent to the park *(100 W. Lafayette St.; 815-433-6100; www. cityofottawa.org/reddick.htm; open year round Mon–Fri 9am–5pm, Sat 9am–4pm, Sun 10am–2pm).* The Reddick Mansion is can be toured *(telephone to book)* and is also hired as a venue for meetings, weddings, wedding receptions and other events.

Indiana Dunes National Lakeshore★

40mi south of Chicago via I-94/ I-90 to I-90; exit at US-20/US-12. Follow US-12 to the lakeshore sites. Visitor information: 219-926-7561; www.nps.gov/indu.

Looking for a brawnier beach than Chicago offers? Then head south to this 25-mile sliver of pristine land wedged around the heavy industry of northern Indiana.

Indiana Dunes National Lakeshore

National Park Service

Indiana Dunes State Park

1600 North 25 East, Chesterton, Indiana. 219-926-1952. www.state.in.us/dnr/park lake/parks/indianadunes.html. Open year-round daily 7am–11pm. $8/vehicle ($4/ vehicle for Indiana residents). Ensconced within the greater national lakeshore, the state park offers 3 miles of beachfront and 16.5 miles of trails. Amenities here include a bathhouse/pavilion, picnic areas and a visitor center.

It's about a 40-mile drive, but don't let the intervening smokestacks deter you; the 15,000 acres of windswept beaches, dunes, marshes and forests of this National Lakeshore are worth the trip. Though brawny they may look, these ancient glacial dunes form a fragile ecosystem at the mercy of prevailing winds, pounding waves and human encroachment. The effort to preserve them began in 1911 and continues to this day.

Mount Baldy

National Park Service

Bailly Homestead and Chellberg Farm and Trail★

On Mineral Springs Rd., 6mi east of Inland Marsh. Open year round 8am–dusk.

Though access to these historic buildings is limited to a few occasions a year, a trek around the two-mile trail here reveals a glimpse of early settlement as well as the natural wonders of the dunes.

Mount Baldy★

One of the largest (123 feet) dunes in the park, Mt. Baldy is constantly being pushed inland by the winds, at a rate of 4 to 5 feet a year. The walk up and around the dune to the beach is short (*.5mi*) and very steep. And no, that massive tower you see is not a nuclear

plant, but a garden-variety power-plant cooling tower.

West Beach Area★

Turn left on County Line Rd., shortly after entering the park. Open May–Sept daily 9am–9pm. Rest of the year daily 8am–dusk. $6/car mid-May–end of Sept. Pets prohibited. Beware of dangerous undertow.

Known primarily for its popular West Beach, this large section of the park also includes Long Lake and 3.5 miles of hiking trails. A walk along the **Dune Succession Trail★** offers a look at the park's surprising biological diversity, encompassing 1,400 plant species.

FOR FUN

Residents of "The City of Big Shoulders" may work hard, but they play hard, too. Chicagoans have a great sense of fun, and they love to share it with visitors. What else would you expect from the folks who brought you The Second City (see p118), the Ferris wheel and the Tootsie Roll? So go ahead, have some fun, Chicago style.

Navy Pier★★

600 E. Grand Ave. at Lake Michigan. 312-595-7437. www.navypier.com. Open May–Aug Sun–Thu 10am–10pm, Fri–Sat 10am–midnight. Sept–Oct & Apr Sun–Thu 10am–8pm, Fri–Sat 10am–10pm. Nov–Mar Mon–Thu 10am–8pm, Fri–Sat 10am–10pm, Sun 10am–7pm. Attractions have separate admission fees. Shops & restaurants closed Thanksgiving Day & Dec 25.

Navy Pier has enjoyed many lives since it was first built in 1916 as—you guessed it—a passenger and freight terminal. Then it served as a naval training station during World War II and as a campus for the University of Illinois. It has hosted festivals, conventions and trade shows. After a period of disuse, the pier was reborn in

Touring Tip

If you do nothing else, take a walk to the end of the 3,000-foot-long pier for some great skyline and lake views★★. On summer Saturdays and Wednesdays, fireworks light up the night sky over the pier (starting at 9:30pm). See p97 for an array of Navy Pier's kid stuff. For information about getting to Navy Pier, see p15.

1995 as the colorful, bustling and thoroughly touristy place you see today. Many of Chicago's sightseeing cruise ships come and go from here, giving the place a truly nautical atmosphere.

In its 50 acres, the pier offers something for everyone, from high culture (the excellent Shakespeare Theater; *see p123*) to carnival food and fun. If it's raining, duck indoors

South Walkway of Navy Pier

City of Chicago/Willy Schmidt

FOR FUN

87

Carousel on Navy Pier

Navy Pier

to the **IMAX Theater**. Relax amid the palms in the tropical **Crystal Gardens** or grab a bite at one of many eateries *(see box, right)*. Outdoors, the 150-foot **Ferris wheel** beckons. **Chicago Children's Museum★** *(On Navy Pier, see p97.)*

Attend a TV or Radio Show Taping

If it's talk shows you want, you have your choice: Jerry Springer or Oprah Winfrey. Tickets are free, but you must plan ahead to join the studio audience for either of these programs, and you must be at least 18 years of age. Tapings generally take place twice on scheduled days during the season.

Oprah Winfrey Show – *312-591-9222 or www.oprah.com.* Reservations are taken only about a month in advance. Shows are taped August through November and January through May, though days vary week to week. Occasionally, you can snag last-minute tickets by email, so check the website.

Jerry Springer Show – *312-321-5365 or www.jerryspringer tv.com.* Shows are taped September through April on Monday, Tuesday and Wednesday, except during weeks of major holidays. You can also get tickets by mail by writing to the studio at 454 N. Columbus Drive, 2nd Floor, Chicago, IL 60611. For more family-friendly

Gourmet to Grub: Dining at the Pier

Though the fare here is on the touristy side, you'll find a variety of styles and lots of kid-friendly food. Lively **Joe's Be-Bop Café & Jazz Emporium** *(312-595-5299)* serves up southern barbecue and traditional live jazz. **Bubba Gump Shrimp Co. & Market** features, well, shrimp and a lot of artificial "atmosphere" *(312-252-4867; www.bubbagump.com)*.**Charlie's Ale House** offers pub surroundings, complete with 70 beers and a list of single-malt scotches, as well as a family-friendly menu *(312-595-1440)*. For fast food, head to the food court, McDonald's, the beer garden (with free live music) or the **Haagen Dazs Café** for sandwiches and oh-so-rich ice cream. You'll find terrific upscale seafood, steak and pasta at **Riva**, which also offers more casual dining at its first-level bar *(312-644-7482)*.

Getting Tickets Before You Go

Individual Cubs' game tickets generally go on sale in late February for the season ahead. When tickets are released, you can purchase them online at the Cubs' website *(http://chicago.cubs.mlb.com)* or at *www.tickets.com (call 800-843-2827 in Illinois, or 866-652-2827 outside Illinois)*.

If You Strike Out . . .

There's more local baseball to enjoy:

Chicago White Sox – American League, Chicago. *312-674-1000 or 866-769-4263. www.chisox.com.*

Kane County Cougars – Class A Affiliate of the Oakland Raiders, Midwest League. *630-232-8811. www.kccougers.com.*

fun, try: – **Wait, Wait Don't Tell Me**, *10 S. Dearborn St. http://chicagopublicradio.org. $21.99.* NPR's news quiz is taped in Chicago live most Thursdays. You wouldn't think watching live radio could be this amusing.

Catch a Cubs Game at Wrigley Field

1060 W. Addison St., at Clark St. From downtown, take Lake Shore Dr. north and turn left on Irving Park Rd.; then go west on Clark St. 773-404-2827. http://chicago.cubs. mlb.com.

There are a lot of sporting events you could enjoy in Chicago, but there's only one **Wrigley Field★** *(see p43)*. Nestled into a busy residential neighborhood on Chicago's North Side, the field languishes sleepily until baseball season when the joint really starts jumping. Cubs' games sell out quickly, despite the fact that the team hasn't won a World Series in a century. During the season, fans jam neighborhood streets and bars for hours before and after each game.

The park seats just over 39,000; seating on the rooftops of neighboring buildings can be reserved for groups *(www.ballparkrooftops. com)*. If you can't get into a game, try one of the ballpark tours offered on Saturdays and Sundays during baseball season *(no tours on game days; 773-404-CUBS; http://chicago. cubs.mlb.com $25)*.

Wrigley Field

©4x6/iStockphoto.com

FOR FUN

Take a Tour of Chicago

Chicago offers a wealth of different tours for every taste. Here's a sampling:

Untouchable Tours – *773-881-1195. www.gangstertour. com. Tours depart from the corner of Clark & Ohio Sts., year-round Sun–Fri 10am & 12pm (also 2pm Sun and 2pm & 7:30pm Fri), Sat 9am, 11am, 1pm, 3pm, 5pm, 7pm (Sat Oct–mid-May 10am, 12pm, 3pm, 5pm, no 2pm Sun; $27).*

No image of Chicago is more popular, or enduring, than the city as a hotbed of gangsters. Even though Al Capone and his cronies are long gone, you can still tour the notable and notorious landmarks of hoodlumdom, including the site of the St. Valentine's Day massacre, and the **Biograph Theater**, where John Dillinger was shot. Costumed guides conduct these two-hour bus tours in character for a lighthearted look at Prohibition-era Chicago.

Chicago Neighborhood Tours – *312-742-1190. www.chicago neighborhoodtours.com. Tours depart from the Chicago Cultural Center, 77 W. Randolph St. Reservations required. $30 adults; children $25, includes refreshments.*

One good way to explore some of the Windy City's more than 130 neighborhoods is on a Chicago Neighborhood Tour, offered by the City of Chicago. Visit historic **Bronzeville** and the South Side, the soul of Chicago's African-American community, or **Uptown**, home of the city's oldest jazz club. Or discover the ethnic flavors of enclaves like Little Italy, Greektown or Chinatown.

Each tour is offered only a few times a year, so check schedules before you go.

Chicago River Tours – See p42.
Ghost Tours – *888-GHOST-91. www.chicagohauntings.com. 600 N. Clark St. $28 adults, $20 children.* See the supernatural side of the city, lead by a local author. The tours include as much history as they do scary stories.

Untouchable Tours

Untouchable Tours

Festival Fun at the Lake

The temperature isn't the only thing that's cooler by Lake Michigan.

The annual **4th of July party** (held the evening of July 3) along the downtown lakefront attracts more than a million people. The spectacular fireworks show, set off from barges just outside Monroe Street Harbor, starts at dusk. The city celebrates **Venetian Night** in late July with a parade of illuminated vessels in Monroe Harbor *(8:30pm)*, followed by fireworks over the water set to rock music broadcast on WXRT (93FM). The **Chicago Air and Water Show** attracts 2 million gawkers in August to see the daredevil jet-powered Thunderbirds and acrobatic stunt flyers duck and dodge high rises at incredible speeds. *For more information, see www.cityofchicago.org/specialevents.*

MUST DO

OUTDOOR FUN

With beaches along Lake Michigan and green spaces galore, Chicago claims plenty of places to play outdoors. So grab your bike, your volleyball, your golf clubs or your ice skates—whatever the season, you won't run out of things to do.

Outdoor Fun in Millennium Park★★★

Bounded by Michigan Ave., Randolph & Monroe Sts. and Columbus Dr. 312-742-1168. www.millenniumpark.org. Open year-round daily 6am–11pm. See p61.

Arriving by bike? Park it, at no charge, at the **McDonald's Cycle Center** *(Randolph St. & Columbus Drive; 888-245-3929; www.mcdonaldscyclecenter.com). A daily pass for secure parking and access to showers and lockers costs $10 for ten days.* During summer festivals and music events, valet bike parking is free! McDonald's Cycle Center also rents bikes by the hour, day or week, and there's even an on-site repair shop and snack bar. Guided bike/walk tours are offered in spring and fall *(see website).* For wintertime fun in the park, try out those figure-eights at the **McCormick Tribune Ice Rink** *(opposite page).*

Oak Street Beach★★

Along the lakefront from 7600 Sheridan Rd., at Howard St., to 9500 E. Ewing Ave., at Calumet Beach. 312-747-0832. www.chicagoparkdistrict.com.

Okay, it's not the Riviera, but Chicago's beaches are sandy, sunny and beautiful. More than 30 of them line the lakefront from north to south, and lifeguards are on duty

Lakefront beach

Chicago Park District

from Memorial Day to Labor Day *(9am–9:30pm).* Some, like the Rogers Park beaches at the north end of the city, are no bigger than a block wide. Others, such as North Avenue Beach and 63rd Street Beach, have bathhouses, concessions and other amenities, as well as large stretches of sand. Several beaches feature nature trails, others have tennis courts and volleyball set-ups. The best sands to see and be seen? That would be **Oak Street Beach** *(access via tunnels at Oak or Division Sts.),* where the tanned and toned soak up rays and swim in the shadow of the Drake Hotel *(see pp30, 140).*

Park Grill

11 N. Michigan Ave. 312-521-7275. www.theparkgrill.com.
For that après-skate dinner, try the rinkside Park Grill, a wood-trimmed, white-tablecloth restaurant serving an upscale American menu. During the summer, the Grill expands into Chicago's largest alfresco-dining venue. You can also reserve picnic bags to go.

Touring Tip
Lake Michigan can be cold, especially in the spring, but the swimming is pleasant and refreshing. If swimming is restricted because of high bacteria counts in the water, lifeguards will post warning signs.

Iceskating in downtown Chicago

©Jim Jurica/iStockphoto.com

Go Skate

Chicago's long, cold winter has some good points: it sets the scene for some great ice skating opportunities.

The city has nine outdoor rinks *(open late Nov–late Feb)* where you can practice your double axels. Some are listed below *(for a complete list, contact the Chicago Park District: 312-742-7529 or www.chicagoparkdistrict.com)*.

- **McCormick Tribune Ice Rink at Millennium Park** – *Michigan Ave. between Washington & Madison Sts. 312-742-5222. Open daily 10am–10pm.* Bring your own blades and skate free of charge, or rent skates *($9).*
- **Daley Bicentennial Plaza** – *337 E. Randolph St., in the Loop. 312-742-7650. Open Mon–Fri 10am–3:30pm & 7pm–9pm, weekends 8:30am–noon. $2 adults, $1 children under age 14. Skate rentals $2 adults, $1 children.*

Gotta grind? Crave a carve? Check out one of Chicago's two permanent street skateparks: 20,000 square feet each of fast concrete fit for old- and new-school skaters alike:

- **Wilson Skatepark** – *Wilson Ave. & Lake Shore Dr.*
- **Burnham Skatepark** – *31st St. & Lake Shore Dr.*

Hit the Links

Chicago Park District courses: 312-245-0909. www.cpdgolf.com. Open year-round (weather permitting) daily dawn to dusk.

The Chicago Park District has six golf courses, three driving ranges *(open 7am–10pm)*, two miniature-golf courses and three learning centers spread across the city. Daily fees vary from $10 to $21 (slightly higher on weekends) and tee times can be reserved online or by phone. *For a list of courses and details, see www.cpdgolf.com.*

The Green: Putting in Grant Park

Tucked away in an old bus turnaround on Monroe Drive between Lake Shore Drive and Columbus Avenue, this 18-hole putting course *(daily 10am–10pm)* features lush plantings, great views and downtown convenience.

At par 42, it offers players a chance to practice their short game with a true-golf experience. It's fun for beginners, too. Enjoy lunch, dinner or snack at The Green's full-service patio restaurant. Call for reservations and tee-times *(352 E. Monroe St.; 312-642-7888; www.thegreenonline.com).*

MUST DO

FOR KIDS

Okay, you've done the architecture, the museums and the historic sites. Now what about the kids? Or the kid in you? Here are some Chicago spots the whole family can enjoy.

Art Institute of Chicago★★★

111 S. Michigan Ave. 312-443-3600. www.artic.edu/aic. See p44.

Begin your family visit to the AIC on the lower level in the **Kraft Education Center**, where kids are invited to get up close and personal with art. Drop-in workshops and craft programs are offered, and the museum also fills a calendar with children's events that require pre-registration. In the **Touch Gallery**, you can do just that, which is, of course, strictly forbidden elsewhere in the museum. Next door, explore the **Thorne Miniature Rooms★★**, tiny handcrafted

Touring Tip

To prepare for a visit to the Art Institute with children, check out the museum's website *(left)* for activities and suggestions on how the kids can have fun with art.

rooms from 68 periods and places around the world. Like fancy dollhouses, each room is furnished on a scale of 1 inch to 1 foot, right down to the rugs and silverware. Up one flight, in the long hall that connects the museum's two wings, fans of long ago and far away will dig displays of arms and armor, swords and scabbards.

Field Museum of Natural History★★★

1400 S. Lake Shore Dr. 312-922-9410. www.fieldmuseum.org. See p46.

Dinos and mummies and bugs, oh my! What more could a kid want? Though much of this museum is geared for older kids and adults, there are some notable highlights for younger visitors—**Sue★★**, the 47-foot-long T-rex, topping the list. For more prehistoric beasts, head to the upper level of the East Wing, where the **DinoZone★★**

Dino Zone, Field Museum of Natural History

©The Field Museum

FOR KIDS

93

Animal Encounters at
Shedd Aquarium

©Shedd Aquarium

exhibit will delight with skeletons of long-necked *Apatasauras*, horned *Triceratops* and the winged *Pteranodon*. On the ground level, **Underground Adventure★** simulates the dark, creepy-crawly world beneath our feet. Your young ones may also enjoy **What Is an Animal?** and **Inside Ancient Egypt**. Kids with special interests in nature and animals could spend all day at the Field.

Shedd Aquarium★★★

1200 S. Lake Shore Dr. 312-559-0200. www.shedd.org. See p49.

This place is a winner with kids of all ages. Brightly colored sea crea-tures captivate little ones, while bigger kids focus on sharks and piranhas and octopi. As you enter, check in the Kovler Family Hall for locations of **Animal Encounters** *(daily 11:30am & 2:30 pm)*, where kids go one-on-one with snakes, tarantulas or frogs. On Tuesdays, you'll find events for preschoolers (ages 3–5) posted there as part of the **Tots on Tuesdays** program, which includes story times, crafts, animal touch programs, music, and characters in costume. And, of course, neither you nor the kids will want to miss the **Marine Mammal Presentations** in the **Oceanarium★★** or feeding time at the **Caribbean Reef★**.

Hooray for Kayavak!

As you visit the Oceanarium, keep your eyes peeled for Kayavak, a special beluga whale with a white birthmark on her back. The whale's mother died of an infec-tion when Kayavak was only five months old. Because the calf was nursing, this might have meant death for her, too. But keepers at the aquarium were deter-mined to keep Kayavak alive. They weaned her to solid food (fish), hoping that she'd be able to make the transition. At least two human companions remained with her 24/7 for the next year. When the time finally came to introduce her to the other whales, they refused to accept her. The scene was painful to watch, but necessary if Kayavak was to live as a normal beluga. One morning, the trainers arrived to find Kayavak swimming together with the pod. Now five years old, she still ranks lowest in the hierarchy, but she's tough and feisty and gets along fine.

All Hands On!

In **Ships Through the Ages**, kids can man the wheel of a 19th century tall ship. To experience liftoff, climb aboard the model **space shuttle** in the Henry Crown Space Center; and for a realistic flight experience, brave the F-14 Tomcat simulators in **Navy: Technology at Sea★** on the main floor. In **Petroleum Planet**, you can even "drive" racecars.

Museum of Science and Industry★★★

57th St., at S. Lake Shore Dr. 773-684-1414. www.msichicago.org. Open year-round Memorial Day–Labor Day Mon–Sat 9:30am–5:30pm, Sun 11am–5:30pm. Rest of the year Mon–Sat 9:30am–4pm, Sun 11am–4pm. Closed Dec 25. $13 adults, $9 children (ages 3–11). Free admission days vary by season. Additional charge for Omnimax Theater & special exhibits. By bus, take the #6 Jackson Park Express bus south to 56th St. and walk one block south. In summer, the #10 MSI bus runs right to the museum. Or take Metra train to 57th St. Station and walk east two blocks.

There's a lot here for kids—and adults—to love, and we mean a lot. Here are some of the most popular kid stops. *For more on the MSI, see p48.*

Toymaker 3000, Museum of Science and Industry

Scott Brownell/Museum of Science

Musts at the MSI

Coal Mine★★ – *Main floor.* A favorite here since 1933, this 20-minute guided tour plunges you from the top of the "headframe" to the "depths" (only a floor down) of a replica coal mine by elevator.

Imaging: Tools of Science★★ – *Main floor.* Computers invite you to manipulate images of your face, create art, and solve crimes.

Toymaker 3000★★ – The best part about this exhibit, intended to teach kids how to create and run a business, is watching a 2,000-square-foot robotic assembly line manufacture 300 tops an hour.

Fairy Castle★ – Furnished with over 1,000 miniatures, the jewel-encrusted Fairy Castle even has running water and electricity. The castle is chock-full of references to familiar fairy tales. Can you find the Bluebird of Happiness?

Heart Balcony★ – Withstanding the test of time since 1952, the exhibit's 16-foot-tall Walk-Through Heart shows how the beat goes on within us. The heart now forms the centerpiece for an updated exhibit on cardiac health.

U-505 Submarine★ – Presented in a spectacular setting that explains the history and context of World War II in the North Atlantic Ocean, this German U-boat is the

FOR KIDS

95

museum's prized artifact. Clever multimedia presentations and compelling films and images rarely seen chronicle the story of its capture off the coast of French West Africa in 1944. Your timed ticket admits you inside the sub, designed to house 56 enlisted men and 4 officers.

Transportation Zone★ – You'll find many of the museum's large vehicles on the main floor, including a cutaway of an actual **Boeing 727★**. The newest star of the gallery is **The Great Train Story★**, where model trains chug around a 3,500-square-foot layout that simulates the busy rail commerce between Chicago and Seattle. Be sure to stop at **All Aboard the Silver Streak★** on the ground floor as you leave for a tour of the **Pioneer Zephyr**, the sleek passenger train that took the West by storm from 1934 to 1960.

Chick Hatchery – Young and old alike are fascinated by watching baby chicks peck their way out of their eggs. Part of the exhibit, Genetics–Decoding Life, the Chick Hatchery is located on the main floor, next to the Transportation Zone.

Idea Factory – *Ground floor; entry by free timed tickets are available at the exhibit entrance.* Very young kids will enjoy this 8,000-square-foot area, loaded with toys and tools for a good time, including a fabulous moat that encircles the space. Next door, 22,000 hand-carved miniature mechanical figures make their way around the **Circus** exhibit.

Henry Crown Space Center – Home of the **Omnimax Theater** *(purchase advance tickets online or by calling the museum)*, this wing also houses the **Apollo 8 command module★**, the first spacecraft ever to circle the moon (1968).

Pioneer Zephyr, Museum of Science and Industry

Scott Brownell/Museum of Science and Industry

Navy Pier

Navy Pier

Navy Pier★★ for Kids

600 E. Grand Ave. at Lake Michigan. See p87. For information about free trolleys to Navy Pier, see p15.

If you can keep them out of the candy and ice cream shops, Navy Pier has rides and amusements that will entertain kids for hours. It won't be cheap, though—each attraction charges its own admission fee. The **Ferris wheel**, a pier landmark, soars up 150 feet, and can sway in the wind on the city's signature windy days. For more excitement, the **Wave Swinger** slings riders through the air. For young kids, there's the old-fashioned **carousel** with its 36 colorful animals. For some really cheesy fun, try Amazing Chicago's Fun-house Maze or the Time Escape 3D Ride, both of which use special effects to transport you through Chicago as you'll never see it again. The Pier also features a mini-golf course and a Build-A-Bear Workshop, for making stuffed animals. The **Chicago Shakespeare Theater** *(312-595-5600; www.chicagoshakes.com; see p123)* often mounts children's productions.

Chicago Children's Museum★

312-527-1000. www.chichildrensmuseum.org. Sun–Wed 10am–5pm, Thu–Sat 10am–8pm). Closed Thanksgiving Day & Dec 25. $9. Free admission Thu after 5pm and first Mon of the month (for children only).

The Children's Museum greets visitors as they enter Navy Pier on foot. There's lots to do here for the under-11-year-old set. Three floors of hands-on exhibits invite youngsters to build bridges and forts, invent a flying machine, dig up dinosaur bones, meet giant insects, explore a replica schooner, and even appear on TV. Programs, performances and workshops (along with happy kids) make this museum a lively place.

Brookfield Zoo★★

8400 W. 31st St., Brookfield. 14mi west of Chicago. 708-688-8000. www.czs.org. Open Memorial Day–Labor Day daily 9:30am–6pm. Rest of the year Mon–Fri 10am–5pm. $11 adults, $7 children ages 3–11. All-in-One tickets include

Brookfield Zoo

major attractions at the zoo: $22.50 adults, $16.50 children ages 3–11. Inquire about free days.

If you have a day to spend, it's worth the jaunt to this suburban zoo. Its 216 acres fan out around a central fountain, and 15 miles of footpaths wind through the lovely grounds. Shady stretches of lawn invite picnicking. With over 2,800 resident beasts, you'll find all your favorites here, from aardvarks to zebras. Here are several exhibits you and the kids shouldn't miss.

Brookfield Breakdown

Seven Seas★★ – Make a beeline in the morning for the Dolphinarium to see a **Dolphin Presentation★** *(several 20min performances*

daily; $2.50 adults, $2 children). Later shows tend to get crowded.

Tropic World★★ – Inhabited by primates, this area offers a dramatic treetop perspective of life in the rainforests of Asia, Africa and South America.

The Fragile Kingdom★ – Clouded leopards, comical meerkats and naked mole rats occupy habitats that re-create an African desert and an Asian rain forest.

Habitat Africa!★ – Wander from the open savanna to the dense forest, admiring giraffes, okapis, crocodiles and pythons en route.

Regenstein Wolf Woods – Brookfield's newest habitat, located in the southwestern corner of the zoo, is home to a pack of endan-

---

Theater for Kids

These Chicago theaters love kids and kids love them back. Here's a quick overview of a few favorites.

Chicago Kids Company – *773-205-9600. www.chicagokidscompany.com.* The company puts on fun plays for kids at various venues.

Emerald City Theatre Company – *773-529-2690. www.emeraldcitytheatre.com.* Emerald City offers Cinderella, Wizard of Oz and the like, usually performed at the Apollo Theater.

Lifeline Theatre – *6912 N. Glenwood Ave. 773-761-4477. www.lifelinetheatre.com.* This small neighborhood theater often brings classic kids' books to life.

Vittum Theater – *1012 N. Noble St. 773-342-4141. www.vittumtheater.org.* Serious and comic theater performances here are tailored to young audiences.

gered Mexican gray wolves. The pack is most active at the beginning and the end of the day.

Lincoln Park Zoo★★

2001 N. Clark St. 312-742-2000. www.lpzoo.org. Open Apr–Oct: grounds open daily 9am–6pm; buildings and farm until 5pm. Nov–Mar: grounds until 5pm, buildings and farm until 4:30pm. Memorial Day–Labor Day weekends and holidays grounds close 7pm, buildings close 6:30pm. Free.

In addition to its wonderful penguin and bird houses, bear and cat habitats and sea lion pool, this accessible zoo's approach is toward replicating environments and encouraging natural animal behavior. From snakes to polar bears, this zoo has it all, and the **Pritzker Family Children's Zoo** is designed to make children feel at home with creatures ranging from snakes to wolves.

Lincoln Park Lineup
Regenstein Center for African Apes★★ – Gorillas and chimps cavort in their 29,000-square-foot indoor-outdoor home. Watch

Touring Tip
To get to the zoo by car from downtown, drive west on I-290 to the First Avenue exit, then continue south on 1st Avenue to 31st Street and follow signs to the main North Gate parking lot *($8)*. By train, take the Burlington Northern Metra train line from Union Station in the Loop. Get off at the zoo stop at Hollywood Station and walk north two blocks *(fares & schedules: 312-836-7000; www.metrarail.com)*. A good way to see the sprawling zoo is via the 45-minute **Motor Safari Tour** *($3 adults, $2 children)*.

them play on 5,000 feet of vines, fish for treats in "termite" mounds and scramble around the mud banks. Beware: they're watching you, too. They love to shoot bursts of air at visitors with a giant air gun!

You will find the Lester E. Fishing Center at this building, where all ages can come and learn interactively about wildlife conservation and related initiatives.

Regenstein African Journey★★ – There's a habitat around every corner here, each one part of an

Lincoln Park Zoo

Lincoln Park Zoo

African ecosystem—we dare you to step into a dark enclave filled with 10,000 Madagascar hissing cockroaches! Outdoors you can wander through the African savanna where the big guys—giraffes, elephants, ostriches—live, or take the **African Safari Ride** *($5)*. On the beautiful **carousel** installed atop the education center, kids can ride their favorite endangered animals *($2.50; open Mar–Oct 10am–4:40pm)*.

Farm-in-the-Zoo Presented by John Deere★ – Here kids can climb aboard a tractor, meet the animals, and feed and milk the cows *(check posters for schedules)*.

🦴American Girl Place

835 N. Michigan Ave. 877-247-5223. www.american girl.com. Open year-round Mon–Thu 10am–7pm, Fri 10am–9pm, Sat 9am–9m, Sun 9am–7pm. Closed Thanksgiving Day & Dec 25.

Little girls and their dolls flock to this full-service fantasyland. After you shop the complete line of

Touring Tip
You can park for $12 along Cannon Drive to the east of the grounds *(enter from Fullerton Ave.)*. Pick up maps, audio tours or strollers in the **Gateway Pavilion** to the north of the main entrance off Cannon Drive. You might also find free parking in Lincoln Park along Stockton Drive to the zoo's west. CTA bus routes 151 and 156 both serve the zoo. If you want to ride around the zoo, hop aboard the **LPZOO Express** *($2.50)*. Park Place Café offers good eats year-round in a food-court setting; or check out Big Cats, Landmark or Elephant cafes for quick bites in the warmer months. Step outside zoo boundaries to the south for a meal at **Café Brauer** *(see p66)*.

American Girl dolls and products (including dress-alike clothing for doll and child), the exhibits, cooking classes, theater programs and reading groups can keep you busy for the rest of the day *(many events require reservations)*. The café *(reservations recommended)* serves brunch, lunch, tea and dinner; special packages are available for birthday parties.
Dolls can even have their hair done in the Doll Hair Salon.
For little girls who love their dolls, a trip to AGP is perfect.
Try to catch a performance of *Circle of Friends, An American Girls Musical.*

American Girl Place

American Girl Place

City of the Big Pizzas

Chicago is one of the country's greatest spots for 'za; aficionados rave about the local deep-dish variety. This savory concoction of tomatoes, cheese, sausage and vegetables ladled over a thick, doughy crust was developed in the 1940s by restaurateur Ike Sewell, whose restaurants **Pizzeria Uno** *(29 E. Ohio St.; 312-321-1000; www.unos.com)* and **Pizzeria Due** *(619 N. Wabash St.; 312-943-2400; www.unos.com)* still serve the genuine article to crowds of eager eaters. Be prepared to wait; cooking your massive pizza takes around 45 minutes.

ComedySportz4Kidz

929 W. Belmont Ave. 773-549-8080. www.comedysportz.com. Sat 2pm (50min show). $8.

Chicago is known for improv comedy. Unfortunately for parents, improv often goes blue, and is typically inappropriate for little ones. ComedySportz has solved that problem, with G-rated shows that actually are funny enough that they don't bore grown-ups.

ESPN Zone

43 E. Ohio St. 312-644-3776. www.espnzone.com/chicago. Open year-round Sun–Thu 11am–11pm, Fri 11am–midnight, Sat 10am–midnight.

Sports fans of all ages will revel in this digital-generation sports bar/arcade. On the second floor, the 10,000-square-foot Sports Arena offers tons of interactive sports and virtual-reality games ranging from bowling to car racing to sky-diving. The third-floor Screening Room is equipped with a 16-foot, high-definition TV and surrounding monitors for the ultimate in multigame viewing.

Swedish-American Museum and Children's Museum of Immigration

5211 N. Clark St. 773-728-8111. www.samac.org. Open Tue–Fri 10am–4pm, Sat–Sun 11am–4pm. $4 adults, $3 children, $10 family rate. Free admission second Tue of the month.

Though tiny from the outside, this Andersonville museum provides hours of entertainment for kids (ages 3–12) in its **Children's Museum of Immigration**. The hands-on facilities give kids a realistic, yet entertaining, look at what it meant to come to the new country, complete with a 20-foot immigrant steamer and a pioneer log cabin. Pre-America takes include a Viking ship and a refugees' raft. Grown-ups can tour the museum's collection of Swedish artifacts and artwork, and shop in the gift shop.

Mitchell Museum of the American Indian

See p57.
3001 Central St., Evanston.

FOR KIDS

SHOPPING

Forget any doubts you may have about Chicago's fashion sense: you can shop this town 'til you drop. Add a dose of Midwestern good sense and practicality, a touch of innovation on a manageable scale, and you have a city where high-style boutiques rub elbows with bargain basements, vintage treasure troves and farmers' markets.

Magnificent Mile★★★

Beverly Hills has Rodeo Drive, New York has Madison Avenue, and Chicago has the Mag Mile. North Michigan Avenue is indisputably *the* shopping promenade in the city. As you stroll the lovely avenue from the river to **Oak Street★** *(see opposite page)*, you'll notice that Mag Mile has fallen victim to the homogenizing effect of contemporary retailing—chain stores like **Crate and Barrel**, **Williams-Sonoma**, **Banana Republic** and **Gap** now mingle with the exclusive boutiques and historic architectural façades. Even so, time spent shopping here will certainly not disappoint the acquisition-minded. Who could resist tony Dallas retailer **Neiman Marcus** *(737 N. Michigan Ave.; 312-642-5900; www.neimanmarcus.com)*? Then there's **Filene's Basement** *(830 N. Michigan Ave.; 312-482-8918; www.filenesbasement.com)*, the country's oldest off-price department store; Swedish fave **H&M** *(840 N. Michigan Ave.; 312-640-0060; www.hm.com)*; and **Niketown Chicago** *(669 N. Michigan Ave.; 312-642-6363; www.niketown.nike.com)*, which offers clothing for every sport along with seasonal celeb appearances. **Crate and Barrel** may be a chain, but it is Chicago's chain, with local roots. Check out their flagship store *(646 N. Michigan Ave.; 312-787-5900; www.crateandbarrel.com)*.

Mag Mile Malls

Vertical malls add scores of stores and restaurants to the possibilities along North Michigan Avenue (malls below are listed from south to north).

North Bridge – *520 N. Michigan Ave. 312-327-2300. www.theshopsatnorthbridge.com*. Fifty shops, 20 restaurants, five hotels, and a four-level shopping center (Nordstrom) fill this attractive mall, where the third floor is devoted exclusively to kids. This is the home of the Seattle retailer **Nordstrom**, which made the Chicago scene in 2000.

600 North Michigan Shops – *600 N. Michigan Ave. 312-266-5630*. Eddie Bauer is a highlight here, along with a multiplex movie theater.

Chicago Place – *700 N. Michigan Ave. 312-266-7710. www.chicagoplace.com*. **Saks Fifth Avenue** anchors these eight levels, which include **Ann Taylor** and **Talbots**. Drop by delightful **Chiaroscuro**, a gallery of colorful, funky eclectica, with items you can't find everywhere else.

Water Tower Place★ – *835 N. Michigan Ave. 312-440-3166. www.shopwatertower.com*. Water Tower Place boasts the largest selection of all, from department-store chains Macy's and Lord & Taylor to trendy **Custo-Barcelona** and **#1 Blue Engine**, devoted exclusively to Thomas the Tank Engine.

New Maxwell Street Market

Canal St. at Roosevelt Rd. Park for $3 at Clinton St. & 14th Pl. Open year-round Sun 7am–3pm. 312-922-3100. Chicago's oldest outdoor market dates back to the late 19th century when Jewish immigrants ran a bustling open-air bazaar here. Although the market and its vendors and shoppers have changed over the years, the place always remained gritty and urban. Today, urban renewal has taken its toll, and the new, sanitized Maxwell Street Market is but a shadow of its former self. Still, more than 480 vendors peddle their wares—from produce to antiques—and street performers and musicians entertain.

The 900 Shops – *900 N. Michigan Ave. 312-915-3916. www. shop900.com.* Swankest of the Mag Mile malls, 900 North Michigan includes a six-story **Bloomingdale's**, plus **Gucci** and **Lalique** among its 70 stores. Other favorites at this landmark establishment include Alternatives hoes *(www. altshoes.com)*, a great source for hip shoes, and Mark Shale *(www. markshale.com)*, the locally owned option for classic workwear for both men and women.

Magnificent Shopping Streets

Oak Street★ – *West side of Michigan Ave., one block north of Walton Pl.* Hunting for haute couture? Duck down Oak Street, where you'll flush out a wonderful array of designer boutiques, jewelry stores and intimate shops. Bag the hippest fashions at **Ultimo** *(no. 114; 312-787-1171; www.ultimo.com)* and **Prada** *(no. 30; 312-951-1113; www.prada.com)*, or shoot for quintessentially elegant accessories at **Hermès of Paris** *(no. 110; 312-787-8175; www.hermes. com)*. At **Frette** *(no. 41; 312-649-3744; www.frette.com)*, the high thread counts of the shop's fine Italian linens reflect equally high prices. Anchoring all this glamour is **Barneys New York** *(no. 25;*

312-587-1700; www.barneys.com). Buyers beware: these trendy shops are not for the faint of budget. One exception is the fabulous **Bravco** *(no 43; 312-943-4305; www.bravco beauty.com; pay by cash only)*. This two-story beauty supple show has brands of beauty products at cheaper prices, but without that icky outlet feel. Perhaps the only other Oak Street bargain is the **Daisy Shop** *(67 E. Oak St., 312-943-8880; www.daisyshop.com)*, a consignment store with a good stock of gently used designer clothes.

State Street★ – *Between Randolph & Adams Sts.* Chicago's first retail corridor, State Street's fortunes in the Loop have soared and dipped

Bloomingdale's on North Michigan Avenue

© Bloomingdale's, Chicago

SHOPPING

103

over the years. For years that Great Street housed two of Chicago's most famous homegrown retailers. That's no longer the case.

The former the flagship Marshall Field's is now **Macy's★** *(111 N. State St.; see p26),* and the former home to Carson, Pirie, Scott & Company Store *(1 S. State St.; see pp23)* is now the Sullivan Center, which is being renovated.

Armitage Avenue – *Between Halsted St. & Racine Ave.; lincolnparkshopping.com.* Stroll this historic district, with its lovely residences, boutiques and eateries. Stop by **Tabula Tua** *(1015 W. Armitage Ave.; 773-525-3500; www.tabulatua.com)* for luscious table settings and other home accessories. Chicago womenswear by **Lori's Designer Shoes** *(824 W. Armitage Ave.; 773-281-5655; www. lorisshoes.com)* for selection and price. Locals also flock to **Fox's De-signer Off-Price** *(2150 N. Halsted St.; 773-281-0700; www.foxs.com),* which offers exactly what its name says. **Mint Julep** *(1013 W. Armitage Ave.; 773-296-2997)* is a funky local clothing boutique. There is no question that you'll be the only person on your block with your

handbag if you buy it at **1154 Lill** *(904 W. Armitage Ave.; 773-477-5455; www.1154lill.com),* because you'll design your own. 1154 has purse patterns and fabrics and ships you your own-of-a-kind creation once it is sewn. In recent years this strip has evolved from local boutiques to nationally-known outposts. You'll find designers like **Cynthia Rowley** *(808 W. Armitage Ave.; 773-528-6160; www.cynthiarowley.com)* and **Barneys New York COOP** *(2209 N. Halsted St.; 773-248-0426; www.barneys.com).*

Southport Avenue – *Between Belmont Ave. & Irving Park Rd.* When local boutiques got priced off of Lincoln Park's Armitage Avenue *(see left)* they fled to Lakeview's Southport Avenue, which has become one of the city's best shopping areas. For close to a decade **Krista K** *(3458 N. Southport Ave., 773-248-1967, kristak.com)* has been the strip's favorite stop for fashion-able women's clothes and, now, maternity clothes, too. Men opt for **Ciao Bella** *(3829 N. Southport Ave.; 773-388-2201)* and there's something for everyone at funky **Uncle Fun** *(1338 W. Belmont Ave.; 773-477-8223; www.unclefunchi cago.com),* right around the corner on Belmont Avenue.

Clark Street – *Between Foster & Bryn Mawr Aves.* Swedish in its origins, **Andersonville** *(www. andersonville.org)* has grown popu-lar and eclectic in its shopping opportunities; you'll find antiques, hip and chic home accessories and gifts here. For a Scandinavian fix, drop by the gift shop at the **Swedish-American Museum Center** *(5211 N. Clark St.; 773-728-8111; www.samac.org; see p101),*

Macy's

Swedish American Museum

The Swedish American Museum

loaded with Kosta Boda crystal and other Swedish specialties. If you have room for furnishings in your suitcase, or you are willing to have things shipped, you cannot miss **Scout** *(5221 N. Clark St.; 773-275-5700; www.scoutchicago.com)* for a well-edited antique décor. **Haus** *(5405 N. Clark St.; 773-769-4000; www.hauschicago.com)* has contemporary art and décor items that are made in small quantities. Reward all your hard retail work (or buy a gift for the housesitter at home) at **bon bon** *(5410 N. Clark St.; 773-784-9882; www.bonbonchicago.com)*, a chocolate shop with treats made in offbeat shapes like Buddha. **Women and Children**

First *(5233 N. Clark St; 773-769-9299; www.womenandchildrenfirst.com)* is not just a bookstore, rather it is a neighborhood icon with plenty of authors' readings, as well as a remarkable selection of books for women and kids.
Damen and Milwaukee Avenues – *Between Webster & Division Aves.* Much of the trendy retail action of artsy **Bucktown/ Wicker Park** happens along Bucktown's Damen and Milwaukee Avenues. Try **p.45** *(1643 N. Damen Ave.; 773-862-4523; www.p45.com)* for edgy women's fashion from Chicago's best young designers. Local designers shine bright at **Eskell** *(1509 N. Milwaukee Ave.; 773-486-0837; eskell.com)*.
Robin Richman *(2108 N. Damen Ave.; 773-278-6150)* is a local dress designer with an eponymous boutique and a terrific eye.
Viva La Femme *(2048 N. Damen Ave.; 773-772-7429; www.vivelafemme.com)* is a rare bird: a store designed for curvy and plus-size women that is hip and fashionable and fun. Walls and walls of color-coordinated ribbon deck the halls at **Soutache** *(2125 N. Damen Ave.; 773-292-9110; soutacheribbons.com)*. It is a

Farmers' Markets

Chicago prides itself on its neighborhood farmers' markets, which bring the bounty of the surrounding countryside into the city from May through October *(check at www.egov.cityofchicago.org for times and locations)*.

Foodies should check out **Chicago's Green City Market** *(1750 N. Clark St., at Stockton Dr., in Lincoln Park; open mid-May–Oct Wed 7am–1pm; 773-435-0280; www.chicagogreencitymarket.org)*. This nonprofit market was created to support the sustainable and organic food movements in Chicago and to provide fresh local produce to an increasing number of restaurateurs. Operating since 1999, the Green Market is open to the public and features at least 50 vendors of heirloom fruits and vegetables along with cooking demonstrations by prominent local chefs.

SHOPPING

paradise for crafty types. Shop for 18th and 19th century Chinese furniture at **Pagoda Red** *(1714 N. Damen Ave.; 773-235-1188; www.pagodared.com)*.

Division Street – *Particularly the 1900 block*. Boutiques and funky shops line the main thoroughfare of nearby **Ukrainian Village**. Locals make a habit of going to **Habit** *(1951 W. Division St.; 773-342-0093; www.habitchicago.com)*, possibly the best boutique for independent designers in town. **Nina** *(1655 W Division St.; 773-486-8996; www.ninachicago.com)* has a minimalist aesthetic, setting it apart from almost any other yarn and knitting store you've entered. **The Ruby Room** *(1743-45 W. Division St.; 773-235-2323; www.ruby room.com; see p111)* is a spa with an impressive retail spa section. Come here for alternative skin care and make-up products, as well as books, crystals and even quirky items like dog collars that change color based on your pup's mood.

Devon Avenue – *Between Western & California Aves.* The "Midwest capital of gold dealers" contains nearly 20 jewelers selling mostly 22- and 24-karat gold jewelry. Bisecting the heart of Chicago's Indian and Jewish communities, Devon also features Indian restaurants and sari shops (with colorful silks) to the east, and farther west, purveyors of all things Judaica, including the famous **Rosenblum's World of Judaica** *(2906 W Devon Ave.; 773-262-1700; www.alljudaica. com)*. Parking is tough in this area at night, but the energy and the great people-watching opportunities make up for any frustration. Shops tend to be open late here.

Wentworth Avenue – *South of Cermak Rd., in Chinatown.* A wonderful place to while away the afternoon, Chicago's **Chinatown** offers shops, groceries, bakeries and restaurants aplenty. Stores carry the usual interesting mix of American, Chinese and Japanese goods, including silk

Chinatown

Brigitta L. House/Michelin

bathrobes, jackets and traditional dresses, ceramics, tea and toys.

Woks 'n Things (2234 S. Wentworth Ave.; 312-842-0701) stocks an amazing array of cookware. Be sure to roam the blocks west of Wentworth for more shops.

Lincoln Avenue – *Between Lawrence Ave. & Montrose Ave.*

Lincoln Square *(www.lincolnsquare.org; see p33)* was once the enclave for German immigrants to Chicago. There are still vestiges of that population here, but its shopping reaches out to a much more diverse crowd. Stop at **Quake Collectibles** *(4628 N. Lincoln Ave.; 773-878-4288)* for nostalgic items form your youth, including action figures and lunch bozes. **The Dressing Room** *(4635 N. Lincoln Ave.; 773-728-0088; www.thedressingroomchicago.com)* has quickly become a must-shop for local women. **Traipse** *(4341 N. Lincoln Ave.; 773-935-5511; www.traipseshoes.com)* stocks high-end, yet comfortable and wearable imported shoes. Sweet-smelling soaps and body washes are just part of the appeal at neighborhood icon **Merz Apothecary** *(4716 N. Lincoln Ave.; 773-989-0900; www.smallflower.com)*. On-staff pharmacists help you make sense of the alternative health and beauty projects stocked here. Take a load off your feet at the **Book Cellar** *(4736 N. Lincoln Ave.; 773-293-2665; www.bookcellarinc.com)*, a combination bookstore and wine bar.

River North Galleries

The **River North Gallery District** *(bounded on the east and west by N. Wells & N. Orleans Sts., and on the south and north by W. Huron St. & W. Chicago Ave.)* vies with Manhattan's Soho for claiming the largest concentration of art galleries. Clustered along and around Superior Street, galleries, antique shops and home-furnishings stores—many of which occupy 19th century warehouses—provide the perfect setting to find that piece of art that you just can't live without. On certain Friday evenings each month, galleries open their new shows *(for schedules check online at www.chicagogallerynews.com or pick up a free copy of Chicago Gallery News)*. If you're adding to your contemporary art collection, here's a few galleries to get you started:

Book Cellar

Book Cellar, Chicago

Andrew Bae Gallery – *300 W. Superior St. 312-335-8601. www. andrewbaegallery.com*. Andrew Bae specializes in contemporary and young Asian artists.

Carl Hammer Gallery – *740 N. Wells St. 312-266-8512. www.hammer gallery.com*. "Outsider" and self-taught artists are featured here.

Catherine Edelman – *300 W. Superior St. 312-266-2350. www. edelmangallery.com*. This is one of the Midwest's leading galleries devoted exclusively to photography.

Marx-Saunders Gallery, Ltd. – *230 W. Superior St. 312-573-1400. www.marxsaunders.com*. Contemporary studio glass and sculpture fill the display space at Marx-Saunders.

Perimeter Gallery – *210 W. Superior St. 312-266-9473. www. perimetergallery.com*. Perimeter offers contemporary painting, sculpture, works on paper and master crafts.

Zolla/Lieberman Gallery – *325 W. Huron St. 312-944-1990. www.zollaliebermangallery.com*. The first gallery to come to River North, in 1975, showcases contemporary works by emerging and established artists.

West Loop Galleries

Douglas Dawson's move of his eponymous **Douglas Dawson Gallery** *(400 N. Morgan St.; 312-226-7975; www.douglasdawson. com)* from River North to the West Loop is one of the things that proved to people that the West Loop was for serious galleries and collectors. Today is it an enclave for avant garde galleries as well as those who simply decided to stop paying River North prices. As in River North, there are open gallery

strolls on Friday nights, usually the first Friday of the month. Stop at Douglas Dawson for some of the best ethnographic art in the country. Fans of glass must shop at **Function + Art** *(1046 W. Fulton Mkt.; 312-243-2780; www. functionart.com)*, a contemporary furniture studio with affordable custom-made works. Across the street (and up a flight) is ground zero for pop art: **Mars Gallery** *(1139 W. Fulton Mkt.; 312-226-7808; www.marsgallery.com)*. Down the block the **Linda Warren Gallery** *(1052 W. Fulton Mkt.; 312-432-9500; www.lindawarrengallery.com)* exhibits emerging artists who aren't often shown in Chicago. Next door, **Morlen Sinoway** *(1052 W. Fulton Mkt.; 312-432-0100; www. morlensinoway.com)* sells furniture, jewelry and gifts as well as fine art). Check your calendar before you visit the neighborhood: If the dates and times line up, both the **Chicago Antique Market** *(1340 W. Washington St.; www.chicago antiquemarket.com)* and Leslie **Hindman Auctioneers** *(1338 W. Lake St.; 312-280-1212; www.leslie hindman.com)* are good places to find one-of-a-kind treasures, often for bargain prices.

South Loop

For too long the South Loop was just somewhere south of all the action, but nowhere you'd want to go. Now, it is a vibrant neighborhood, a destination in its own right. One of the strengths is the bookstore mecca that is Printers Row. Try **Sandmeyer's Book Store** *(714 S. Dearborn St.; 312-922-2104)* and **Printers Row Fine and Rare** *(715 S. Dearborn St.; 312-583-1800)*. Other growth has come in the University Village end of the neighborhood. Those who prefer yarn to paper flock to knitting shop **Knitwerks** *(1934 S. Wabash St.; 312-949-9276; knitwerks.net)*. The neighborhood is also home to **Southgate Market** *(1101 S. Canal St.)*, a sustainable shopping center. **Flaunt Boutique** *(75 E. 16th St.; 312-360-1000)* is the neighborhood favorite for women's clothing, and no one can resist buying gifts at **Hazel** *(921 S. Loomis St.; 312-733-2227)*. **Lush Wine & Spirits** *(1306 S. Halsted St.; 312-738-1900)* is a great alternative to fussy wine shops. Those with a penchant for shoes ought to check out the selection at **Heelz** *(69 E. 16th St.; 312-235-0467)*.

Hyde Park

Hyde Park's academic roots, thanks to the University of Chicago, shine through when it comes to shopping. While there is plenty of diversity, the strength of the neighborhood shopping is its bookstores, both new and used. Your first stop must be **Seminary Co-op Bookstore** *(5757 S. University Ave.; 773-752-4381)*, chock-full of any book you could want and many more that you've never heard of. Owned by the same fine folks who own Seminary, **57th Street Books** *(1301 E. 57th St.; 773-684-1300)* it has more general interest and children's books. **Powell's Books** *(1501 E. 57th St.; 773-955-7780)* is for those who prefer used books, and the treasure-hunting process of finding them. Every good college town/ neighborhood has a good place to buy music. For Chiago, here it is: **Dr. Wax Records & Tapes** *(5225 S. Harper; 773-493-8696)*.

Bargains at Outlet Mall Shopping

If you have access to a car and really want a bargain, consider driving to one of several outlet malls in the greater Chicago area. All of them have stores from major national designers at discount prices, some with more in-season goods than others.

Clothes

For the best selection of designer clothes, try **Chicago Premium Outlets Mall** *(1650 Premium Outlets Blvd., Aurora; 630-585-2200)*. **Gurnee Mills Outlet Mall** *(6170 W. Grand Ave., Gurnee; 847-263-7500)*, which has something for everyone, including the perk of being across the street from an amusement park. There are play areas, movie theaters and other entertainment in addition to shopping.
Prime Outlets Huntley Mall *(11800 Factory Shops Blvd., Huntley; 847-669-9100)* – Though smaller than Chicago Premium, this place also has designer clothing and home décor shops.

Local stores with outlets

Some local stores also have their own outlets in the city, including furniture heavyweight **Crate & Barrel** *(1864 N. Clybourn Ave.; 312-787-4775)* and **Madison and Friends Outlet** *(1963 N. Halsted St.; 312-943-0436)*, which stocks denim for kids and tweens.
Dish towels and table lines can be scooped up at the Tag brand outlet, **1730 Outlet Company** *(1730 W. Wrightwood Ave.; 773-871-4331; www.1730outlet.com)*.

SHOPPING

SPAS

Need a vacation from your vacation? Chicago has just the thing. Slip away for a couple of hours—or make a day of it—and indulge yourself at one of the city's many pampering palaces.

Asha

55 E. Ontario St., Magnificent Mile. 312-664-0200. www.ashasalonspa.com.

Asha has become the Aveda spa heavyweight in Chicago, with six locations in the city and suburbs, including on the Gold Coast and in Bucktown. A favorite indulgence is the location at the **James Chicago** *(see p141)*, where the service is even more attentive than usual. Despite the chain's size, you are sure to get personalized care here. Weary travelers who struggle with keeping healthy on airplanes should try the sinus-friendly Neti Massage.

Charles Ifergan

106 E. Oak St., Magnificent Mile. 312-642-4484. www.charlesifergan.com.

This establishment was among the first businesses on Oak Street, and today its friendly staff offers expert salon and spa services. Whether you get the works in a Day of Beauty or just go for a two-hour Executive Treatment, you'll emerge feeling like a whole new person.

Elizabeth Arden Red Door Salon and Spa

919 N. Michigan Ave. (enter on Walton St.), Magnificent Mile. 312-988-9191. www.reddoorspas.com.

The grand dame of all spas, and the classic choice of Chicago's most pampered, Elizabeth Arden's tony Red Door delivers skin care, massage, hydrotherapy and more with panache. Try an Elemental Balancing massage, in which aromatherapy oils are custom blended for you.

Exhale

945 N. State St., Gold Coast. 312-753-6500. www.exhalespa.com.

This light-filled spa near Oak Street is all luxury. Whether you are looking for beauty treatments, spa treatments or some serious yoga instruction, Exhale is the place to relax and take a deep breath. **Note:** Exhale is popular with locals, so call as far ahead as possible to make appointments.

Nurture in Nature

Ensconced in beautiful Illinois farm country, **Heartland Spa** is a healthy jaunt from Chicago, but worth the trip if you'd like to concentrate a few days on improving your fitness through exercise, diet and stress relief *(90 miles south of Chicago, off I-57 South; 1237 E. 1600 North Rd., Gilman, IL; 815-683-2182 or 800-545-4853; www.heartlandspa.com)*. You can take aerobic and strength classes, tai chi and yoga, and enjoy a full range of body treatments.

Masage at Exhale

Exhale Spa, Chicago

🔥 Kiva Day Spa

196 E. Pearson St.,
Magnificent Mile. 312-840-8120.
www.premierspacollection.com.

Spa aficionados may recognize Kiva's parent company, the Premier Collection of Spas, with locations coast to coast. In Chicago, the southwestern surroundings are relaxing and welcoming. In addition to standard spa services, Kiva offers reflexology, cocoon therapies (choose from Ayurvedic, marine, mother earth and more), and treatments for men.

Mario Tricoci

900 N. Michigan Ave.,
Magnificent Mile. 800-874-2624.
www.tricoci.com.

Big, bold cousin of the **Red Door** (both are owned by Elizabeth Arden), Tricoci has locations all over the Chicago area, particularly in the suburbs. This huge facility offers everything from Spa-on-the-Go to the MT Signature Day of Beauty, among other packages. Or choose polishes, wraps, massages, hair, make-up and nail services à la carte.

Paradise Sauna

2910 W. Montrose Ave.,
Lincoln Square. 773-588-3304.

A traditional Korean spa, Paradise is not fancy by any stretch of the imagination. But the hot and cold dipping pools and well-trained massage therapists make this a great place for some hard-core R&R for both men and women (in segregated areas).
Note: You must pay the fee to use the pools if you come for a treatment (massage and body scrubs), so you should plan on using them.

Peninsula Spa

108 E Superior St.,
Magnificent Mile. 312-573-6860.
www.peninsula.com.

Those who are serious about being pampered know to turn to one of the most luxurious hotels in the city for one of its most luxurious spa experiences. This is not for the budget-minded.
Note: Everything at the Peninsula is pricy, although worth it if you like to indulge. Favorites include couples massages in your hotel room as well as treatments near the mosiac-adorned pool. Keep your eyes open: You may see some celebrities here.

The Ruby Room

1743-45 W. Division St.,
Ukrainian Village. 773-235-2323.
www.rubyroom.com.

This is a high-end spa with a holistic attitude. If you are curious about alternative therapies, but have been wary, this is a great place for a first-time treatment. Choose from massage and skin

SPAS

treatments or more esoteric energy healing. Your interest in and comfort level with the New Age material guides the staff.

Spa Space

161 N. Canal St., Near West Side. 312-466-9585. www.spaspace.com.

This spa caters to busy professionals and offers a full line for men (Space Men, that is), including sports pedicures and back facials. With advance warning, meals or snacks can be ordered from restaurant Nine's spa menu, and the spa has its own juice bar.

Thousand Waves Spa for Women

1212 W. Belmont Ave., Lakeview. 773-549-0700. www.thousandwavesspa.com.

For women only, this serene, Japanese-style spa offers massages provided by women trained in a variety of techniques. Herbal wraps come in flavors from white pine bark to rosebud. All treatments begin in the three baths—dry sauna, eucalyptus steam and Jacuzzi sauna. If you only want to access the baths, no appointment is needed.

Urban Oasis

Micheal Lapin/Urban Oasis

Tiffani Kim Institute

310 W. Superior St., River North. 312-260-9000. Also in Park Hyatt Hotel, 800 N. Michigan Ave., Magnificent Mile; 312-335-1234. www.tiffanikiminstitute.com.

Tiffani Kim Institute

Tiffani Kim Institute

A smorgasbord of therapies, body treatments and relaxation awaits you at one of Tiffani Kim's two locations (the Park Hyatt spa includes a hair salon). Couples, best friends, and moms and daughters can book specialty services for two, such as facials and massages. And, the Institute even has a line of services for teens, both boys and girls. If you're in the market for a bridal gown, check out Tiffani Kim's stunning line of original designs.

Urban Oasis

939 W. North Ave. (garden level), Old Town; 312-640-0001. Also at 12 W. Maple St. (3rd floor), Gold Coast; 312-587-3500. www.urbanoasis.biz.

Massages are the order of the day here; from reiki and shiatsu, to hot-stone and deep-tissue, you'll find whatever your tired body needs. Try the salt glow, an exhilarating exfoliation treatment, followed by a 30-minute massage.

MUST DO

NIGHTLIFE

The blues rule in Chicago, and jazz is vice-president. There are plenty of venues to hear both, as well as other types of music—reggae, rock, house and hip-hop. Dance, drink, lounge to your heart's content, upscale or down. Oh, and there's a little comedy club here called **The Second City**, along with others in both stand-up and ensemble style.

Blues Clubs

Blue Chicago

736 N. Clark St.; 312-642-6261. Also at 536 N. Clark St.; 312-661-0100. www.bluechicago.com.

One cover charge gets you into both Blue Chicago clubs, just blocks apart from each other in River North. These newcomers are not your typical funky blues clubs, but they do offer good music. On Sunday afternoons, you can catch an all-ages blues concert at the Blue Chicago Store *(534 N. Clark St.; 312-661-1003).*

B.L.U.E.S.

2519 N. Halsted St., Lincoln Park. 773-528-1012. www.chicago bluesbar.com.

You feel as though you can reach out and touch the performers in this tiny, smoky club. Quality musi-cians from across the city and a down-and-dirty atmosphere make this one of the most popular blues bars in town.

Buddy Guy's Legends

754 S. Wabash Ave., South Loop. 312-427-0333.

Blues headliners take the stage here around 10:30pm, but earlier audiences on Friday and Saturday are treated to free acoustic sets beginning at 6pm.

House of Blues

329 N. Dearborn St., River North. 312-923-2000. www.hob.com.

Blues is big business here, along with classic rock, heavy metal and other genres. Try the Gospel Brunch with two seatings every Sunday *(9:30am & noon)* for a rockin' good time.

© Mark Montgomery/City of Chicago

Blue Chicago

NIGHTLIFE

Singin' the Blues

Born in the dusty cotton fields of the Mississippi River delta, the musical genre called the Blues evolved from African slave chants, work songs and spirituals into a uniquely American musical form. From the hollows, fields and churches of the rural South, migrants brought their music north to Chicago in the 1910s. As artists such as "Big Bill" Broonzy and "Papa" Charlie Jackson began to play together, a hybrid guitar-driven style based on urban themes emerged. In the 1940s musicians experimented with amplification, and by 1950 Chicago surfaced as the capital of the hard-driving electric blues, with Muddy Waters (McKinley Morganfield) as its king. Today, Chicago greats like Willie Dixon, Koko Taylor, Buddy Guy and others push the blues into the 21C.

Kingston Mines

*2548 N. Halsted St.,
Lincoln Park. 773-477-4646.
www.kingstonmines.com.*

Frequented by top-notch musicians and regular folk, this ramshackle blues club features live music until 4am (5am on Saturday). Every night, two top local bands take turns playing on the club's two stages. The place fills up quickly, and at 2am fans pour in from B.L.U.E.S. across the street, so arrive early to get a good seat.

Jazz Clubs

Andy's Jazz Club

*11 E. Hubbard St.,
Magnificent Mile. 312-642-6805.
www.andysjazzclub.com.*

This one's a classic, and it offers jazz three times a day: at lunch, the cocktail hour and mid-evening. The food's not bad here, either.

Cotton Club

*1710 S. Michigan Ave.,
South Loop. 312-341-9787.*

Dress up and step out for some cool jazz in the Cab Calloway Room or an "urban contemporary" DJ mix in the Gray Room.

Green Dolphin Street

*2200 N. Ashland Ave., Bucktown.
773-395-0066.*

This big, swanky dinner-and-dance spot features the best of both worlds. Expensive meals are served in the cool dining room, and diners are invited to stay and enjoy jazz (with lots of Latin) in the roomy club for a discounted cover charge. Or just come for the music; the joint starts jumpin' after 10pm.

Green Mill Jazz Club

*4802 N. Broadway Ave., Uptown.
773-878-5552. www.greenmill
jazz.com.*

Al Capone's crew used to hang out in this charming jazz club; the interior looks much as it did back in the 1920s and 30s. Jazz acts perform seven nights a week, and

Green Mill Jazz Club

Green Mill Jazz Club

MUST DO

Pops for Champarge

Pops for Champagne

the music plays until 4am (5am on Saturday). On Sunday evenings, thick-skinned poets read their works to the crowds who attend the infamous Uptown Poetry Slam competitions.

Joe Segal's Jazz Showcase

47 W. Polk St., The Loop. 312-360-0234. www.jazzshowcase.com.

"Where Jazz Lives in Chicago"—and how. Since 1947 Joe's been bringing jazz stars to his stage to the delight of Chicagoans. There's even a Sunday matinee where kids get in free *(4pm).*

New Checkerboard Lounge for Blues 'n' Jazz

5201 S. Harper Ct., Hyde Park. 773-684-1472. www.checkerjazz.org.

This is the new, re-opened location of a long-time Hyde Park (and Chicago) favorite. As its name suggests, you'll hear blues and jazz, and some of the best in the city at that. Names like Prince and Keith Richards played at the old Bronzeville location. That may not be happening in Hyde Park, but the club still attracts talented

musicians. Expect a diverse crowd, from young to old, thanks to the proximity to the University of Chicago campus. Sundays are a jazz bargain at $10 (cash only).

Pops for Champagne

601 N. State St., Magnificent Mile. 312-266-7677. www.popsfor champagne.com.

Elegant and sophisticated, but not snooty, Pops makes for special nights out. With more than 100 champagnes and live jazz every night, a fireplace in winter and a store where you can shop for bubbly to take home, Pops sparkles for appetizers or dessert. On the North Side, visit the **Star Bar** *(2934 N. Sheffield Ave., Lakeview. 773-472-7272).*

The Velvet Lounge

67 E. Cermak Rd., Near South Side. 312-791-9050.

Blink and you'll miss this wonderful little bare-bones club, which offers excellent jazz Wednesday through Sunday nights. Don't blink, though, because you do not want to miss it!

115

Jimmy's Woodlawn Tap

1172 E. 55th St., Hyde Park.
773-643-5516.

This dimly lit tavern is the off-campus hangout for University of Chicago types. Jimmy's prices are low, the beer selection is good and the bartenders are friendly, so drop by for a cold one (and live jazz on Sunday nights).

Music and Dance Clubs

Double Door

1572 N. Milwaukee Ave.,
Wicker Park. 773-489-3160.
www.doubledoor.com.

This is the premier live music venue in the area. The owners book bands that are just breaking onto the national scene, and the small, V-shaped room is a great place to see future stars up-close.

Empty Bottle

1035 N. Western Ave., Wicker Park.
773-276-3600.

The Empty Bottle books an eclectic mix of experimental jazz, hot local rock acts and bands on the brink of national renown.

Enclave

220 W. Chicago Ave.,
River North. 312-644-0234.
www.enclavechicago.com.

If you want to dance the night away, head to Enclave, a warehouse-turned-dance club with plenty of room on the dance floor and interesting art on the walls. The signature drinks at the bar aren't bad either.

Excalibur

632 N. Dearborn St., River North.
312-266-1944.

Housed in the old Chicago Historical Society, the spacious Excalibur offers something for every-one: eating, dancing, and 12 separate bars ranging over three floors. Music options run from live to DJ, alternative to rock.

Funky Buddha Lounge

728 W. Grand Ave., River West.
312-666-1695. www.funky
buddha.com.

This crowded, too-cool (and possibly too-loud) dance lounge features DJ or live music—jazz, Latin, hip-hop and house—along with a retro-Zen eclectic scene.

Liar's Club

1665 W. Fullerton Ave., Lakeview.
773-665-1110.

It looks like a dive bar from the outside. In fact, one of the city's best, least pretentious nightclubs rages inside. There is a tiny, yet active, dance floor, moving to sounds spun by a DJ. Music ranges from 70s, 80s and 90s tunes, while a disco ball hangs above. The upstairs has a pool table and a more low-key vibe. Expect to pay a $5 cover on weekends.

Lumen

839 W. Fulton Mkt., West Loop.
312-733-2222. www.lumen-
chicago.com.

A nightclub that tries to combine the best of both worlds, Lumen offers a see-and-be-seen atmosphere, but without the VIP sections

Now for Something Completely Different

Several Chicago wine bars do more than just let you sip and sample. Airy and fresh, **Bin 36** *(339 N. Dearborn St.; 312-755-9463; www.bin36.com)* offers unique wine-tasting and cheese flights at its sleek zinc bar. Tastings at **Eno Wine Bar** *(505 N. Michigan Ave.; 312-321-8738; www.enowinerooms.com)* include chocolate as well as vino.

and long lines. The interior is sleek and minimalist and the lights, video and audio are all state-of-the-art. Music tends toward hip hop and dance music. The dress code prohibits ball caps and flip flops.

Metro

3730 N. Clark St., Lakeview. 773-549-0203. www.metrochicago.com.

Metro is not new, having taking up space near Wrigley Field since 1983. But, as other clubs come and go, Metro remains hip. With a mission to bring emerging musical artists to town, it still has its finger on the pulse. See bands ranging from little-known Nashville start-ups to bigger names like The White Stripes and the Yeah Yeah Yeahs. Cover charge depends on the band. Downstairs you'll find **Smart Bar**, an always-packed dance club.

Paramount Room

415 N. Milwaukee Ave., River West. 312- 829-6300. www.paramount room.com.

Part gastropub, part late-night hang-out, this bar (with better-than-average bar food) transforms as the evening wears on. There's a DJ on weekends, and occasionally live music, and always a crowd of locals.

Sonotheque

1444 W. Chicago Ave., Ukrainian Village. 312-226-7600. www.sonotheque.org.

As its name suggests, it is all about the sound at Sonotheque. A well-designed space, with innovative use of acoustical tiles, helps muffle sound in some places and helps the beat go on in others. The club plays an eclectic cross-section of music throughout the week, and hosts racy movie nights and other counter-culture activities.

The Violet Hour

1520 N. Damen Ave., Wicker Park. 773-252-1500, www.theviolet hour.com.

The inspiration for The Violet Hour was the pre-Prohibition Era, and Chicagoans have been flocking here as if there is nowhere else to get a drink other than their own bathtubs. The creative cocktail menu is impressive, but not speedy, as each drink is made with care. This is one of the few clubs in Chicago where it is hard to find the exterior door, although looking for the crowds should be your first clue. The dress code at this speak-easy is relatively basic; no ball caps or cell phones are allowed.

Comedy Clubs

ComedySportz

See p101.
929 W. Belmont Ave.

ImprovOlympic

3541 N. Clark St., Lakeview.
773-880-0199. www.improv
olympic.com.

Primarily a club for aspiring comics, ImprovOlympic features an array of ensemble revues performed by teams of comedians-in-training. Shows run in two theaters seven days a week; some start as late as midnight.

The Second City

1616 N. Wells St., Old Town. 312-337-3992. www.secondcity.com.

What would we do without The Second City? Its satirical improv comedy has shaped the national sense of humor since the televi-sion show *Saturday Night Live* took to the air in 1975.

The troupe was founded in Hyde Park on the city's South Side in 1955 as the Compass Players. Scores of comedians started here, including Alan Alda, Elaine May, Ed Asner, Ann Meara, Joan Rivers and a galaxy of *SNL* stars led by John Belushi, Dan Aykroyd, Gilda Radner and Mike Myers (the voice of Shrek). The hilarity continues with regular no-holds-barred re-vues nightly on the Mainstage, the E.T.C. stage and Donny's Skybox.

Zanies

1548 N. Wells St., Old Town.
Box office 312-337-4027.
www.chicago.zanies.com.
General admission charges start
at $22, but prices vary. Minimum
entry age is 21.

The oldest comedy club in the city (and now the country), this well-worn venue has been running for 30 years and has outlasted a dozen glitzier competitors.
Name any stand-up comedian, and chances are he or she has performed here. The club usually features three comics a night: two up-and-coming performers and a well-known headliner. Zanies also has premises in Main, Nashville, St. Charles and Vernon Hills.

The Second City

The Second City

PERFORMING ARTS

Chicago's theater and performing-arts scene is extraordinarily diverse and accomplished. With over 120 professional theater companies, Chicago offers everything from popular Broadway musicals to gritty "off-Loop" productions. Traditional and contemporary ethnic dance troupes and opera and ballet companies make their home here, and music of all kinds flows nightly. Below are some suggestions for a night at the theater.

Chicago Theater District

Many of the Loop's glorious 19th century movie, vaudeville and stage theaters are gone now, but a few have been preserved and renovated, and new venues have been added. The theaters below are located throughout the Loop, but tend to cluster in the area bounded by Washington Street, Lake Street, LaSalle Street and Wabash Avenue. *Except where noted, you can purchase tickets for the Chicago Theater District venues online at: www.ticketmaster.com.*

Auditorium Theatre

50 E. Congress Pkwy. 312-922-2110. www.auditoriumtheatre.org.

The granddaddy of Chicago's historic theaters, this classic venue, which opened in 1889, makes for theatergoing at its best. Its fine acoustics and lovely, renovated spaces are a delight. Programming varies from local dance troupes such as the Joffrey Ballet *(see p120)* to Broadway musicals.

Cadillac Palace Theatre

151 W. Monroe St. 312-986-5853. www.broadwayinchicago.com.

This lavish venue, inspired by historic French palaces, started out in 1926 as a vaudeville house. It later featured both movies and live stage shows. Renovated and reopened in 1999, the Cadillac Palace now hosts pre-Broadway hits such as *The Producers* and other big-time musicals.

Chicago Theatre

175 N. State St. 312-462-6300. www.thechicagotheatre.com.

Opened as a movie palace in 1921, the glittering Chicago Theatre was resurrected, restored and reopened in 1986. Frank Sinatra performed the opening concert, and today the schedule ranges from Bonnie Raitt to the National Acrobats of Taiwan.

Chicago Theatre

Chicago Theatre

BOX OFFICE

Touring Tip

For up-to-the-minute information and links to Chicago theaters and performing-arts organizations, check out the website of the League of Chicago Theatres: www.theatreinchicago.com.

Gene Siskel Film Center

164 N. State St. 312-846-2600. www.siskelfilmcenter.org.

Founded in 1972 by the School of the Art Institute, the GSFC is a major center of cinematic art and history. The state-of-the-art facility screens new American and foreign films, independent productions and retrospectives.

Goodman Theatre

170 N. Dearborn St. 312-443-3800. www.goodmantheatre.org.

Long located adjacent to the Art Institute, the formidable Goodman Theatre moved in 2000 to this newly constructed home in the Loop. The theater still features classic and contemporary works of serious drama on its two stages.

Out of the Loop

The Loop isn't the only place to see good theater. Other worthwhile venues outside the Loop include the 440-seat **Apollo Theater** *(2540 N. Lincoln Ave.; 773-935-6100; www.apollochicago.com)*, offering lighter musicals and stage works; and the **Athenaeum Theatre** *(2936 N. Southport Ave.; 773-935-6860; www.athenaeumtheatre.com)*, which stages dance, performance groups and theater schools from around the city in its 1,000-seat main stage.

Oriental Theatre/Ford Center for the Performing Arts

151 W. Randolph St. 312-986-6863. www.broadwayinchicago.com.

The "hasheesh-dream décor" of this 1926 theater that delighted silent-movie audiences has been restored for modern theatergoers. Large-scale stage productions such as *Ragtime*, *Fosse* and *Mamma Mia!* make a splash here.

Bank of America Theatre/ Shubert Theatre

18 W. Monroe St. 312-986-6821. www.broadwayinchicago.com.

Bank of America Theatre

Bank of America Theatre

The Shubert was built as the Majestic Theatre, a popular vaudeville venue, in 1906. Along with box-office hits such as *Cabaret* and *Rent*, it's now known for such pre-Broadway engagements as *Sweet Smell of Success* starring John Lithgow, and *Movin' Out*, a collaboration by Twyla Tharp and Billy Joel. In 2005 a $40 million renovation morphed the cramped quarters of The Shubert into a performance space with the décor of old, but the amenities of the 21st century.

MUST DO

Conductor Bernard Haitink leads the Chicago Symphony Orchestra

Todd Rosenberg/Chicago Symphony Orchestra

Music and Dance

Chicago Symphony Orchestra

220 S. Michigan Ave.
312-294-3333. www.cso.org.

Over the last 112 years, the CSO has built a global reputation, which continues under the batons of Music Director Daniel Barenboim and Principal Guest Conductor Pierre Boulez. During the season *(Sept–June)*, barely a night goes by without music at the CSO's new Symphony Center.

Hubbard Street Dance Chicago

Various venues around Chicago. 312-850-9744. www.hubbardstreetdance.org.

For sheer athleticism and exuberance, the 21 dancers in Hubbard Street's main company can't be beat. With a repertoire that blends ballet, jazz, modern and ethnic dance and music into a seamless whole, these performances are always fun.

Joffrey Ballet

Auditorium Theatre, 50 E. Congress Pkwy. 312-739-0120. www.joffrey.com.

Still under the artistic direction of its co-founder (with Robert

Aragon Entertainment Center

1106 W. Lawrence Ave.
773-561-9500.

This 1926 ballroom was built to look like a Spanish village, and it still retains that European charm, all these decades later. In its heyday, names like Tommy Dorsey graced its stage. Today, nestled in the gentrifying Uptown neighborhood, the Aragon is not the crown jewel it once was, but still a gem. The venue hosts many live music concerts, various television progams, boxing and wrestling matches, and it canalso be hired for private functions.
Both English- and Spanish-language stars play here.

Beverly Arts Center

2407 W. 111th St. 773-445-3838.
www.beverlyartcenter.org.

This South Side performance hall has an intimate stage for music concerts, dance and plays.
The center is home to an annual Irish Film Festival and other cinematic events.

Hot Tix
Try snagging half-price, same-day show tickets at one of the Hot Tix outlets *(www.hottix.org)* around the city: 72 E. Randolph St., Loop; 163 E. Pearson St., Magnificent Mile; 9501 N. Skokie Blvd., in Skokie; and at all Tower Records stores.

PERFORMING ARTS

BOX
OFFICE

Joan W. and Irving B. Harris Theater
for Music and Dance

Joffrey), Gerald Arpino, the choreography and programming of this
first-class dance company thrill
audiences year-round.

Joan W. and Irving B. Harris Theater for Music and Dance

*205 E. Randolph St.
312-334-7777. www.
harristheaterchicago.org.*

Opened in November 2003, the
Harris Theater provides a much-
needed home base for Chicago's
midsize music and dance
companies. The interior of this
underground (literally) theater in
Millennium Park may not be glitzy,
but the sightlines and acoustics in
the 1,500-seat space are excellent.
There are other **Millennium
Park★★★** *(see p61)* performing-
arts venues. Curling stainless-steel
ribbons frame Frank Gehry's
state-of-the-art **Jay Pritzker
Pavilion★★★**, host to a variety of
musical performances *(www.mil
lenniumpark.org/events.htm;
see p61).*

Lyric Opera

*20 N. Wacker Dr.
312-332-2244. www.lyricopera.org.*

Chicago's major opera company
occupies the stately Civic Opera
House, which opened in 1929. The
lavish theater seats over 3,500, and
each season includes a classic or
debuting American work.

Muntu Dance Theatre

*Various venues around Chicago.
773-241-6080. www.muntu.com.*

Founded in 1972, Muntu (which
means the "essence of humanity"
in Bantu) performs contemporary
and historic African, Caribbean and
African-American dance and music
that pulse with rhythm and color.

MUST DO

Chicago Theater Companies

Bailiwick Repertory Theatre

1229 W. Belmont Ave. 773-883-1090. www.bailiwick.org.

Anything goes here: From the raucous *Naked Boys Singing!* to Shaw's *St. Joan*, you'll find it all at this theater. The Bailiwick Arts Center boasts a 150-seat main stage, a 90-seat studio and a 40-seat loft.

Chicago Shakespeare Theater

800 E. Grand Ave., on Navy Pier. 312-595-5600. www.chicago shakes.com.

Shakespeare would love the carnival atmosphere of Navy Pier, where this delightful 500-seat courtyard theater stages marvelous interpretations of his works.

Steppenwolf Theatre

1650 N. Halsted St. 312-335-1650. www.steppenwolf.org.

You know their names: John Malkovich, Gary Sinise, William Peterson, Laurie Metcalf and so many others. They all did their early work at Steppenwolf, Chicago's premier off-Loop theater. The 510-seat Downstairs Theatre, the largest of three, features world premieres and new interpretations of the classics with a focus on the ensemble acting that made Steppenwolf famous. Upstairs and in the Garage Theater, emerging artists and new plays rule.

Victory Gardens Theater

2243 N. Lincoln Ave. 773-871-3000. www.victorygardens.org.

Acclaimed for its productions of new and living playwrights, the VGT owns the historic Chicago Landmark building, the **Biograph Theater** at 2433 N. Lincoln Avenue. The VGT expanded this building for use as a live venue and named it Victory Gardens at the Biograph. World premieres are a specialty at Victory Gardens Theater, so be the first on your block to see an exciting new work.

Ravinia Music Festival

200 Ravinia Park Rd., Highland Park. 847-266-5100. www.ravinia.org.
This world-famous outdoor festival spreads out over 36 lush acres in the North Shore suburb of Highland Park. Summer home of the Chicago Symphony Orchestra since 1936, Ravinia today offers everything from jazz, pop and chamber music to folk, dance and children's programs. The complex includes several restaurants, covered pavilion seating, and two indoor theaters. Most fun, though, is to enjoy summertime performances with a picnic dinner on the lawn—with or without candelabra.

PERFORMING ARTS

RESTAURANTS

The venues listed below were selected for their ambience, location and/or value for money. Rates indicate the average cost of an appetizer, an entrée and a dessert for one person (not including tax, gratuity or beverages). Most restaurants are open daily (except where noted) and accept major credit cards. Call for information regarding reservations, dress code and opening hours. For a list of restaurants organized by theme (Special Occasion, Easy on the Budget, etc.), see p138.

| Luxury | **$$$$** | Over $50 | Inexpensive | **$$** | $15–$30 |
| Moderate | **$$$** | $30–$50 | Budget | **$** | Under $15 |

LUXURY

Arun's

$$$$ **Thai**
4156 N. Kedzie Ave., Wrigleyville. Dinner only. Closed Mon. 773-539-1909. www.arunsthai.com.

Reputedly among the best Thai restaurants in the country, Arun's does not offer a standard menu, preferring to serve a 12-course—and popular—prix-fixe menu *($75 and up).*
Against a backdrop of mahogany, Thai silk, wall murals and Thai craftwork, diners here can sample a delightful array of delicacies and flavors selected and blended with exquisite attention to detail. Whereas the six appetizer courses are served one by one, the entrées are served family style.
Choices can range from snapper in red tamarind sauce to "golden baskets," a house specialty of shrimp-and-chicken-filled pastries. The meal ends with Arun's palate-cleansing lemongrass elixir.

Charlie Trotter's

$$$$ **New American**
816 W. Armitage Ave., Lincoln Park. Dinner only. Closed Sun & Mon. Jackets required. 773-248-6228. www.charlietrotters.com.

Tables at the restaurant run by culinary genius Charlie Trotter get booked 4 to 12 weeks in advance. The draw? One-of-a-kind dishes prepared with naturally raised meats, organic produce and vegetable-based sauces. Choose from two daily eight-course prix-fixe menus, the grand dégustation menu *($135)* and the lighter vegetable menu *($115).* For a special treat, reserve the sole kitchen table, where cooking becomes performance.

Everest

$$$$ **French**
440 S. LaSalle St., in One Financial Place, Loop. 312-663-8920. Dinner only. Closed Sun & Mon. www.everestrestaurant.com.

Named for its lofty perch on the 40th floor of the Chicago Stock Exchange, Everest commands a sweeping view of the city. Award-winning chef Jean Joho (also of Brasserie Jo; p126) crafts the finest seasonal ingredients into mouth-watering creations, adding accents from his native Alsace. Order à la carte to sample some of Joho's signature dishes—foie gras terrine, apple and Alsace Tokay gelée; roasted Maine lobster in Alsatian Gewurztraminer butter and ginger—or be adventurous and try the tasting menu *(seven courses for $89)*.

Dining Room, Spiaggia

Levy Restaurants

 L20

$$$$ **Seafood**
2300 N. Lincoln Park West. Lincoln Park. 773-868-0002. www.l2orestaurant.com.

Chef Laurent Gras gained fans in New York and San Francisco (not to mention France) before he moved to Chicago. His seafood-centric restaurant almost immediately had an obsessive following. Housed in the former Ambria space, L20 fuses Japanese and European influences for its fresh-from-the-sea approach. If you can't decide with all the good dishes on the menu, try one of two prix-fixe options: a four-course menu for $110 or a 12-course tasting for $165.

Spiaggia

$$$$ **Italian**
980 N. Michigan Ave., 2nd floor of One Magnificent Mile Building, Magnificent Mile. Dinner only. Jackets required. 312-280-2750. www.levyrestaurants.com.

Overlooking Oak Street Beach and Lake Michigan through its floor-to-ceiling windows on the north end of Michigan Avenue, Chicago's toniest Italian restaurant offers a soaring array of dishes that are well-grounded in regional Italian cuisine. Pastas are handmade; meat and fish are wood-roasted—try the signature Colorado lamb chop with polenta and Brussels sprouts. Next door, dressed-down **Café Spiaggia** *(lunch Mon–Sat, dinner nightly, brunch Sun)* serves tasty pizzas and pastas at more palatable prices.

Tru

$$$$ **New American**
676 N. St. Clair St., Magnificent Mile. Dinner only. Closed Sun. Reservations required. 312-202-0001. www.trurestaurant.com.

At once lush and spare, the dining room at Tru sets the stage for the epicurean theater to follow. Original Warhols and other artworks add color to the room, and the tables are serenely minimalist. After you choose from four prix-fixe menus, the fun begins. Award winning chefs Rick Tramonto and Gale Gand (of Food Network fame) send out course after course, each more exquisite than the last in both food and presentation. These are not large courses, mind you, but jewel-like creations to tease the palate. Dinner takes about three hours when served this way, but it's a lovely, sensual experience.

RESTAURANTS

Bistro 110

Levy Restaurants

MODERATE

Bistro 110

$$$ **French**
*110 E. Pearson St., Magnificent
Mile. 312-266-3110. www.bistro
110restaurant.com.*

The roasted garlic bulb that
accompanies your baguette at this
bright, bustling French bistro sets
the tone for the wood-oven-roast-
ed meats and fish served here—
all redolent with garlic. Good basic
steak au poivre and *steaks frites*
are sure to satisfy, as are bistro
favorites like cassoulet Toulousian
and Robuchon lamb shank, slow-
roasted in its own juices. This is a
great place for a lunch break while
shopping on Mag Mile.

Blackbird

$$$ **New American**
*619 W. Randolph St., Near West
Side. Closed Sun. 312-715-0708.
www.blackbirdrestaurant.com.*

In contrast to its stark white
exterior and minimalist décor, this
tiny Market District hot spot serves
dishes that are a feast for the eyes,
prepared in a style that acclaimed
chef Paul Kahan describes as

"seasonal American with French
countryside influences." The name
Blackbird comes from French slang
for a plump Merlot grape. Try the
signature wood-grilled California
sturgeon, or perhaps a stuffed
breast of bobwhite quail with
medjool dates, lobster mushrooms
and white-corn grits. You never
know what you might find; the
menu and wine list both change
frequently.

Brasserie Jo

$$$ **French**
*59 W. Hubbard St., River North.
Dinner only. 312-595-0800.
www.brasseriejo.com.*

Chef Jean Joho (also of the dressier
Everest; see p124) works magic

Brasserie Jo

Brasserie Jo

with the country fare of Alsace, offering among other hearty dishes a marvelous sausage choucroute, a flaky onion tart, a lobster bouillabaisse, and the restaurant's "Famous Shrimp Bag" (shrimp and vegetables bathed in a light cream sauce and steamed in a phyllo bag). The largely Alsatian wine list, good beer and authentic Parisian brasserie atmosphere complete this delightful dining experience. Bring the kids; they get some surprises along with their own menu.

Green Zebra/Grapevine Public Relations, Inc.
Green Zebra

🍴 Custom House

$$$ Steakhouse
500 S. Dearborn St. Printers Row.
312-523-0200. www.custom
house.cc.

Certainly, Chicago has no shortage of steakhouses. But chef-owner Shawn McClain (Spring, Green Zebra) challenges the genre. Instead of oversized portions of classics, he offers up new interpretations, using local ingredients and a minimalist aesthetic. Not for those who just want a slab of beef, but for those who are ready for a different side of the cow.

🍴 Green Zebra

$$$ Vegetarian
1460 W. Chicago Ave., River West.
Dinner only. Closed Mon.
312-243-7100. www.
greenzebrachicago.com.

Chicago may be prized for its beef, but you couldn't tell it by Green Zebra, which has been packing in crowds of vegetarians since it opened in spring 2004. Named for a variety of heirloom tomato, this hot spot pulses with a hip vibe evident in its buzzing dining room and techno-modern décor. Chef Shawn McClain displays his culinary artistry using the freshest offerings of the season in selections like silky avocado panna cotta with tomato gelée, crème fraiche and sweet corn chips; and cave-aged-gruyère soufflé with endive and heirloom apples. Save room for the white-chocolate dreamsicle, with vanilla-bean ice cream, orange granité and ginger soda.

Harry Caray's

$$$ American
33 W. Kinzie Ave., River North. 773-465-9269. www.harrycarays.com.

Cubs fans will revel in the atmosphere here, which is chock-full of baseball memorabilia and items relating to the Hall of Fame career of late baseball announcer Harry Caray. House specialty chicken Vesuvio (chicken sautéed with garlic, then baked with crispy potatoes and served with peas and a white-wine reduction) and 23-ounce Prime Porterhouse steaks top the menu. The 60-foot-long bar makes a great gathering place. Prices range widely so there's something for everyone.

RESTAURANTS

The Pump Room

$$$ **New American**
In the Omni Ambassador East Hotel, 1301 N. State Pkwy., Gold Coast. 312-266-0360. www.pumproom.com.

In its heyday during the 1940s, this restaurant was the place for Chicago's swell set and visiting Hollywood stars to see and be seen. They undoubtedly came for the outrageous service—dishes were delivered on flaming swords, and guests' dogs could dine in the adjacent Pup Room. While it's no longer the center of Chicago society, the Pump Room remains a charming, elegant restaurant with excellent food. Rumors are it's becoming fashionable again.

Rhapsody

$$$ **New American**
65 E. Adams St., Loop. Closed Sun. 312-786-9911. www.rhapsodychicago.com. No gym shoes, blue jeans or shorts.

Much of the charm of this elegant urban dining spot derives from its location in Symphony Center at the heart of Chicago's Loop, which is framed beautifully in the restaurant's glass window-walls. Eclectic and inventive dishes (Coq au Vin blanc, Nantucket Bay scallops glazed with orange reduction) and desserts worthy of an encore draw on flavors from around the world. Wrap up your meal with the aptly named Chocolate Symphony, a sampling of bittersweet chocolate crème caramel, molten chocolate brownie and white praline hot chocolate. Reserve early on performance nights.

Russian Tea Time

$$$ **Russian**
77 E. Adams St., Loop. 312-360-0000. www.russianteatime.com.

Distinguished by red-velvet furnishings, this elegant (if over the top) tea room located one block from the Art Institute buzzes with the polite chatter of classical-music lovers when the symphony performs. Fine caviar and champagne are de rigueur in the evening as is tea in the afternoon. The restaurant also offers a complete menu for lunch and dinner featuring Russian, Uzbek, Ukrainian and Baltic delicacies. Like Rhapsody,

Rhapsody Restaurant

© Jal Girard

this is another restaurant that's popular with the symphony crowd, so reserve early.

Saloon Steakhouse

$$$ American
200 E. Chestnut St., Magnificent Mile. No lunch weekends. 312-280-5454. www.saloonsteakhouse.com.

There are plenty of good steakhouses in Chicago. It's the atmosphere at the Saloon that sets it apart—more a neighborhood tavern than a swanky steakhouse. The room is small, but comfortable, and the steaks, vegetables and potato sides keep 'em coming back for more. Among its other fine cuts, The Saloon serves Wagyu beef, which is American-raised Kobe-style beef. Added benefits: the service is friendly and the wine list is long.

Tizi Melloul

$$$ Moroccan
531 N. Wells St., River North. Dinner only. 312-670-4338. www.tizimelloul.com.

Wonderful contemporary Moroccan and Mediterranean cuisine is served here amid billowing curtains and pillows in rich reds and golds. Every inch the casbah, Tizi Melloul is a lot of fun. Start with a refreshing Rockin' Moroccan cocktail (vodka, lime juice, fresh mint, soda water and a splash of Sprite), then dive into the fire-roasted mussels. The tagine (lamb and dates stewed in a special clay pot and served over toasted orzo) makes a particularly good entrée. After dinner, lounge in the bar with a nightcap and a hookah. Come Sunday nights to catch the belly dancing.

Tizi Melloul

Tizi Melloul

Topolobampo

$$$ Mexican Regional
445 N. Clark St., River North. Closed Sun & Mon. 312-661-1434. www.fronterakitchens.com.

Chef Rick Bayless has given his sophisticated cuisine a nationwide reputation by the skillful blending of traditional Mexican flavors from Yucatan to Oaxaca. The chef's way with chilies and mole is particularly notable, and fish dishes excel. The menu changes every two weeks, but *puerco en manchamanteles*

Topolobampo Restaurant

Topolobampo

(Maple Creek Farm pork loin in red-chile sauce with plantains, pineapple and homemade chorizo) and *pescado en mole Amarillo* (pan-seared day-boat catch in Oaxacan yellow mole with smoked Prince Edward Island mussels and red-chile rice) are typical of the chef's culinary artistry. You'll find the same quality—at a lower cost—at the more casual **Frontera Grill**, which shares space with Topolobampo.

INEXPENSIVE

17 West at the Berghoff

$$ German
*17 W. Adams St., Loop.
Closed Sun. 312-427-3170.
www.17westchicago.com.*

On the site of what was the 107-year-old beloved German restaurant called The Berghoff, 17 West blends contemporary bistro food with classic German fare. Look for modern takes on sauerbraten, schnitzel and bratwurst. The authentic 19th century atmosphere, such as the carved wood bar, may make you want to linger.

The Century Room, Berghoff Restaurant
© Berghoff restaurant

Andies

$$ Mediterranean
*5253 N. Clark St., Andersonville.
773-784-8616. www.andiesres.com.*

It may be off the beaten path, but if you're shopping in Andersonville (see p33) at lunch or dinnertime, give Andies a try. A nice fireplace warms up the whitewashed room, which is clean and inviting. The menu blends Mediterranean and Middle Eastern flavors into an impressive montage of dishes at very reasonable prices. Ingredients are always fresh, and the service is friendly. Andies also features a kids' menu. You'll find another location a little farther south at 1467 W. Montrose Ave. *(773-348-0654).*

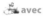 **avec**

$$ New American
*615 W. Randolph St.,
Near West Side. 312-377-2002.
www.avecrestaurant.com.*

It is hard to believe that this small space was once intended to handle the overflow from Blackbird. Instead, now avec, from the same crew that brings you Blackbird, is a destination in its own right. The communal tables are always packed, often with chefs from other restaurants. The strength of the menu is in its simplicity. The house-made charcuterie is legendary.
Note: avec does not accept reservations, so you are likely to wait for a table.

MUST EAT

avec Restaurant

Café Ba-Ba-Reeba!

$$ **Spanish**
2024 N. Halsted St., Lincoln Park.
773-935-5000. www.leye.com.

Though other tapas bars have cropped up since, this was Chicago's original. Seven seating areas decked in bright Mediterranean colors accommodate 360 diners. Ambience and food still sizzle, and the crowds come to enjoy hot and cold tapas ("little dishes" ordered in quantity and shared), paella, and a nice selection of Spanish wines.

Club Lucky

$$ **Italian**
1824 W. Wabansia Ave., Bucktown.
773-227-2300. www.club-lucky.com.

In a neighborhood where eateries come and go, Club Lucky has endured. Generous portions of homestyle Italian cooking—rigatoni with veal meatballs, eggplant parmigiana, shrimp scampi, chicken oreganato—great martinis and a funky 1940s supper-club atmosphere team up to make this lounge/restaurant a long-lived hit.

Erwin

$$ **American**
2925 N. Halsted St., Lakeview.
Dinner only (brunch Sun).
Closed Mon. 773-528-7200.
www.erwincafe.com.

Seasonal specialties with Midwestern flavor grace Erwin's simple but robust menu. Creative vegetable and fruit preparations and savory sauces embellish basics like calves' liver, pan-roasted Great Lakes whitefish, wood-grilled pork chops, and even hamburgers—served with fries, horseradish slaw and homemade pickles. The smallish room is casual yet chic and comfortable, with the cozy feel of a friend's dining room.

Gino's East

$$ **Pizza**
633 N. Wells St., River North. 312-943-1124. www.featuredfoods.com.

Chicago's favorite deep-dish pizzeria, renowned for its two-inch-thick pies and its graffiti-splattered wooden booths, which have been moved to a new location in the space once occupied by Planet

Deep dish pizza at Gino's East

Gino's East

Hollywood. Call ahead and order your pizza, or be prepared to wait at least 30 minutes for your pie to cook.

Heaven on Seven

$$ Cajun
111 N. Wabash Ave., 7th floor of Garland Building, Loop. Breakfast & lunch Mon–Sat. Dinner third Fri of month (reservations required). Closed Sun. 312-263-6443. www.heavenonseven.com.

Creole shrimp, crab cakes, po-boy sandwiches and gumbo are just a few of the New Orleans-style dishes served in this small but bustling lunchroom. Most entrées are served plenty spicy, but connoisseurs of Cajun heat use the bottles of Louisiana hot sauce on the tables to season their food. For a sweet ending, try a healthy serving of cinnamon-spiked bread pudding. A slicker version of the original, **Heaven on Seven on Rush**, is at 600 N. Michigan Ave., 2nd floor *(312-280-7774).*

BUDGET

Ann Sather

$ Swedish-American
909 W. Belmont Ave., Lakeview. No dinner Mon, Tue. 773-348-2378. www.annsather.com.

A welcoming atmosphere and home cooking with a Swedish flair have made this a favorite among Chicagoans since 1945. Breakfast is a specialty—think Swedish pancakes with lingonberries or Swedish meatballs. And be sure to try the homemade cinnamon rolls. Reasonably priced dinner entrées (baked chicken, Tom turkey, Lake Superior whitefish) come with two sides and dessert. Belmont Avenue is the flagship, but Ann Sather also has other locations in Lakeview and Andersonville.

Chicago Pizza and Oven Grinder

$ Italian
2121 N. Clark St., Lincoln Park. Dinner only Mon–Fri, lunch weekends. 773-248-2570. www.chicagopizzaandoven grinder.com.

Located across the street from the site of the St. Valentine's Day Massacre, this nook in the base-

Chicago Pizza & Oven Grinder Restaurant

The Chicago Pizza & Oven Grinder Restaurant

ment of a Victorian brownstone serves unusual topsy-turvy pizzas that resemble potpies. Abundant salads can be shared and the grinders (the local term for submarine sandwiches) are generous. Good food and the laid-back atmosphere make this place popular and the waits sometimes long.

Green Door Tavern

Ed Debevic's

$ **American**
640 N. Wells St., River North.
312-664-1707. www.featured
foods.com.

"Good food, fresh service": that's the mantra of this Chicago institution, known for its sassy waitstaff who talk back and randomly jump up on the counter to sing. Kids and tourists seem to love it, and the diner fare—chili, burgers, hot dogs, meatloaf, ribs, milkshakes and thick malts—isn't bad either.

Gold Coast Dogs

$ **American**
159 N. Wabash Ave., Loop.
312-917-1677.

The Chicago-style hot dog ranks with deep-dish pizza as a source of local culinary pride, and this busy stand serves up some of the best in town. Though topping choices vary depending on individual taste, the Chicago-style dog (known as a "red hot") typically consists of a Vienna beef frank served on a poppy-seed bun. Mustard, relish and onions are a must, and tomatoes, pickle slices, cucumber, lettuce and both green and hot peppers are often added, along with a dash of celery salt. Ketchup, however, has no business on a red hot!

Green Door Tavern

$ **American**
678 N. Orleans St., River North.
312-664-5496.

Constructed only one year after the Chicago Fire of 1871, this is among the oldest downtown buildings and shows its age in a ten-degree list to the right and sloping floors. It's been a tavern since 1921 and today serves good burgers, sandwiches (try the triple-decker grilled cheese), and 35 different kinds of beer.

Half Shell

$ **Seafood**
676 W. Diversey Pkwy.,
Lincoln Park. 773-549-1773.

This quintessential neighborhood dive is located below street level; its downscale atmosphere is at odds with its surroundings. Though small and dark, Half Shell lures loyal locals craving fresh crab legs, shrimp, oysters and fried seafood for lunch or dinner. Diners are welcome to belly up to the curving bar, which takes up half the room, rather than wait for a table.

Healthy Food

$ **Lithuanian**
3236 S. Halsted St., Bridgeport.
312-326-2724.

Don't let the name fool you; they don't serve health food here. What they do offer is yummy Lithuanian home cooking. Traditional folk art decorates the walls and the menu offers a mix of specialties, vegetarian entrées and some American favorites. Breakfast is best and the *blynais* (pancakes served with sour cream), smeared with chunky fruit compote, are to die for.

Hema's Kitchen

$ **Indian**
6406 N. Oakley Ave.,
West Rogers Park. 773-338-1627.
www.hemaskitchen.net.

Hema Potla and her family prepare awesome home-cooked Indian food in her little Far North Side restaurant. The wait can be awesome, too, especially on weekends, so be prepared. You can BYOB to enjoy while you wait. So popular has Hema's cooking become that she's opened another spot in Lincoln Park at 2411 N. Clark Street *(773-529-1705)*.

Lou Mitchell's

$ **American**
565 W. Jackson Blvd,.
Near West Side. 312-939-3111.

The place for breakfast (you can get lunch, too) in downtown Chicago since 1923, Lou Mitchell's still serves up manly portions of oatmeal, eggs, pancakes, French toast and fluffy over-stuffed omelets to satisfy the heartiest

Lou Mitchell's

appetites. Don't mind the plastic plants and the no-nonsense service.

Mr. Beef

$ **Italian**
666 N. Orleans St., River North.
Lunch only Mon–Sat. Closed Sun.
312-337-8500.

Tonight Show host Jay Leno put this place on the map. He discovered it as a struggling stand-up comic working the nightclub circuit and has been recommending it to his Hollywood pals for years. Go to Mr. Beef for the Italian beef sandwiches, consisting of a soft Italian roll piled high with thinly sliced marinated beef garnished with giardinere (pickled peppers, celery and spices).

Mr Beef

The Third Coast

$ American
1260 N. Dearborn St.,
Gold Coast. 312-649-0730.
www.3rdcoastcafe.com.

Sip cappuccino or claret in this warm, comfortable coffeehouse and wine bar, which is open early and into the wee hours. The clientele here ranges from well-dressed Gold Coast matrons to bohemian art students who stay at the Three Arts Club across the street. Good, light fare includes soups, sandwiches and salads. It's a nice place to meet for lunch.

Twin Anchors Restaurant-Tavern

$ Barbecue
1655 N. Sedgwick St.,
Old Town. 312-266-1616.
www.twinanchorsribs.com.

Beloved for its succulent, melt-in-your-mouth ribs, Twin Anchors has been a popular pub since it opened after Prohibition; Frank Sinatra stopped here regularly in the 1960s. The essential neighborhood joint with its relaxed and modest atmosphere makes a nice escape from upscale chic.

Viet Bistro

$ Vietnamese
1346 W. Devon Ave., Rogers Park.
773-465-5720.

The family who was once behind the beloved Pasteur opened this more budget-friendly Vietnamese eatery. While the menu may be easier on the wallet than their previous restaurant, the dishes

are still authentic. Pasteur fans are happy to see the return of whole red snapper on the menu. But Viet Bistro is hipper than Pasteur ever was, with fun tasting events and a creative drinks menu.

Wishbone

$ Southern
1001 W. Washington Blvd.,
Near West Side. No dinner Mon.
312-850-2663. www.wishbone
chicago.com.

Have a heaping helping of hoppin' John or mix and match down-home side dishes with blackened catfish and chicken étoufée. Wishbone's colorful, lively dining room attracts an eclectic crowd, from kids to celebrities, and serves a hearty Cajun breakfast as well. There's another location at 3300 N. Lincoln Avenue *(773-549-2663)*.

Wow Bao

$ Asian
835 N. Michigan Ave., in Water
Tower Place, Magnificent Mile.
312-642-5888. www.wowbao.com.

If you want a quick bite while you're shopping on Mag Mile, Wow Bao serves up fresh steamed buns (bao) to business-lunchers and shoppers alike from their take-out booth just inside the Chicago Water Tower. Asian buns are served hot and stuffed with such combinations as Kung Pao chicken, spicy Mongolian beef, and green vegetables. Wash your selection down with ginger ale made with fresh ginger, or hibiscus iced tea. Rice bowls, salads and soups are also available.

RESTAURANTS

Oak Park/Evanston

Café le Coq

$$$ **French**
*734 Lake St., Oak Park.
708-848-2233.*

This tiny gem has become a destination for Chicago gourmets. The cozy place seats 75 and serves bistro favorites such as mussels in white wine, filet of sole stuffed with shrimp soufflé, and duck à l'orange for two. Service is efficient and friendly, and the atmosphere conjures up late 19th century Paris. The list of French wines (more than 60 labels) includes some good lesser-known vintages.

Campagnola

$$$ **Italian**
*815 Chicago Ave., Evanston.
847-475-6100. www.campagnola
restaurant.com.*

With its emphasis on local and farm-fresh ingredients, a trip to Campagnola is like a little trip to Italy. The cozy space has tables pushed close together. You and your companions will dine on delicacies such as pork chops, pastas and pane cotta. This is a great place for a date or a leisurely night out.

Chef's Station

$$ **American**
*915 Davis St., Evanston.
847-570-9821. chefs-station.com.*

Nestled under the train tracks in Evanston, Chef's Station is easy to walk by. But you shouldn't. It is surprisingly romantic, even with the train whizzing by, and the menu is simple, yet well done.

The flash-fried Spinach is translucent and unusual. Favorite entrées include the lamb, sole and duck breast.

Davis Street Fishmarket

$$ **Seafood**
*501 Davis St., Evanston.
847-869-3474. www.davisstreet
fishmarket.com.*

Forget those warnings you got about not ordering seafood in the Midwest. This unpretentious joint serves delicious, simply prepared fish and shellfish from the ocean, gulf and Great Lakes. Decorated in a funky Key-West-meets-Nantucket style, the fishmarket forsakes haute cuisine for broiled, baked, sautéed, steamed, blackened or fried fish, served with redskin potatoes and corn on the cob.

Davis Street Fish Market

©Scott Shigley 2006/Davis Street Fish Market, Evanston

Tapas Barcelona

$$ **Spanish**
*1615 Chicago Ave., Evanston.
847-866-9900. www.tapas
barcelona.com.*

Colorful and noisy, Tapas Barcelona serves excellent "little plates," paellas, sandwiches and even pizzas with an Iberian flare. Don't miss the *datiles con tocino*, a sinful concoction of baked fresh dates wrapped with bacon in a bell-pepper sauce. Reasonably priced Spanish wines are available by the glass or bottle, along with ports, sherries and other cordials.

Union Pizzeria

Union Pizzeria

Union Pizzeria

$$ Italian
1245 Chicago Ave., Evanston.
847-475-2400. unionpizza.com.

Hip and the suburbs doesn't usually go together. But ever since this sleek pizzeria opened, city-dwellers have been hightailing to Evanston to see-and-be-seen and eat some of the area's best wood-fired pizzas. The restaurant also has an impressive beer and wine list. Union Pizzeria is owned by the folks who brought you Campagnola.

Dixie Kitchen

$ Southern
825 Church St., Evanston.
847-733-9030. www.dixiekitchen evanston.com.

The music is loud and the crowd louder, but what else would you expect from a Cajun place? All the classics are on the menu here:

fried green tomatoes, crawfish, jambalaya, black-eyed peas and gumbo. The restaurant's breakfasts—served seven days a week—are popular with locals. Unlike many classic Southern eateries, Dixie Kitchen does have options for vegetarians.

Hemmingway's Bistro

$ French
211 N. Oak Park Ave., Oak Park.
708-524-0806. www.hemming waysbistro.com.

Step back into the 1930' at this French bistro. Named for the author who was born in Oak Park (despite the misspelling), the eatery offers a seafood bar, plus French classics such as Beef Wellington, Coq au Vin and duck a l'orange. The Sunday champagne brunch is popular.

Petersen's Ice Cream Parlor and Sweet Shoppe

$ Ice Cream
1100 Chicago Ave., Oak Park.
708-386-6131.

Since 1919, Petersen's has been a fixture in Oak Park. If you miss the old time ice cream parlor (and who doesn't), stopping here is essential. Many a child (or disinterested spouse) has been convinced to go on walking tours of Frank Lloyd Wright homes with the promise of Petersen's afterwards. Don't skip the malt milkshake!

RESTAURANTS

RESTAURANTS BY THEME

Looking for the best restaurant for your special occasion?
Want to see that star chef from the Food Network? In the preceding
pages, we've organized the eateries by price category, so below we've
broken them out by theme to help you plan your meals while you're in
town. *Restaurants listed below are in Chicago unless otherwise noted.*

Breakfast Spots
Ann Sather *(p132)*
Healthy Food *(p134)*
Lou Mitchell's *(p134)*
Wishbone *(p135)*

Easy on the Budget
Chicago Pizza and Oven
  Grinder *(p132)*
Ed Debevic's *(p133)*
Gold Coast Dogs *(p133)*
Green Door Tavern *(p133)*
Half Shell *(p133)*
Hema's Kitchen *(p134)*
Lou Mitchell's *(p134)*
Mr. Beef *(p134)*
The Third Coast *(p135)*
Wishbone *(p135)*
Wow Bao *(p135)*

Ethnic Experiences
Healthy Food *(p134)*
Hema's Kitchen *(p134)*
Viet Bistro *(p135)*
Tizi Melloul *(p129)*

Family Places
Andies *(p130)*
Brasserie Jo *(p126)*
Ed Debevic's *(p133)*
Gino's East *(p131)*
Gold Coast Dogs *(p133)*

Hippest Décor
Blackbird *(p126)*
Green Zebra *(p127)*

Neighborhood Favorites
Bistro 110 *(p126)*
Café Le Coq (Oak Park) *(p136)*

Chicago Pizza and Oven
  Grinder *(p132)*
Club Lucky *(p131)*
Erwin *(p131)*
Gino's East *(p131)*
Half Shell *(p133)*
Heaven on Seven *(p132)*

Pre-theater Dining
Rhapsody *(p128)*
Russian Tea Time *(p128)*

Restaurants with History
17 West at the Berghoff *(p130)*
Green Door Tavern *(p133)*
The Pump Room *(p128)*

Special-Occasion Restaurants
Arun's *(p124)*
Charlie Trotter's *(p124)*
Everest (Jean Joho) *(p124)*
Spiaggia *(p125)*
Topolobampo *(p129)*
Tru *(p125)*

Small Plates (Tapas)
Café Ba-Ba-Reeba! *(p131)*
Tapas Barcelona (Evanston) *(p136)*

Star Chefs
Charlie Trotter's
  (Charlie Trotter) *(p124)*
Everest (Jean Joho) *(p124)*
Topolobampo (Rick Bayless) *(p129)*

Steakhouses
Custom House *(p127)*
Harry Caray's *(127)*
Saloon Steakhouse *(p129)*

MUST EAT

HOTELS

The properties listed below were selected for their ambience, location and/or value for money. Prices reflect the average cost for a standard double room for two people in high season. High season in Chicago is summer; rates are considerably less in low season. Price ranges quoted do not reflect the Chicago hotel tax of 15.4%. For a list of hotels organized by theme (Posh Places, Hotels for Business, etc.), *see p153*.

Luxury	$$$$$	Over $350	Inexpensive	$$$	$175–$250
Expensive	$$$$	$250–$350	Budget	$$–$	Under $175

LUXURY

Four Seasons Hotel

$$$$$ 343 rooms
120 E. Delaware Pl., Magnificent Mile. 312-280-8800 or 800-819-5053. www.fourseasons.com/chicagofs.

Done in lush fabrics, dark woods and rich colors, guest rooms wrap visitors in luxury with marble baths and thick terry robes.
On the 32nd to 46th floors of the hotel, deluxe rooms afford sweeping views of Lake Michigan or the city skyline. For business travelers, "Executive-Tech" rooms feature additional data ports and a four-in-one fax machine/copier/scanner/printer. Work out in the large fitness facility, complete with an indoor pool. Once you've tired out those muscles, a trip to the hotel's urban spa might be in order. **Seasons Restaurant ($$$$)** serves contemporary American fare in its opulent dining room; Chicagoans love it for Sunday brunch. Adjoining **Seasons Lounge** is a perfect place for afternoon tea.

The Peninsula Chicago

$$$$$ 339 rooms
108 E. Superior St., Magnificent Mile. 312-337-2888 or 866-288-8889. www.chicago.peninsula.com.

A new addition to Chicago's star-studded hotel lineup, the Peninsula (yes, as in the incomparable Hong Kong Peninsula) is indeed a luxurious stay. Quietly elegant, trim and classic, the hotel is nonetheless futuristic in its many appointments, which include steamless TV screens in the bathrooms. Spacious rooms, among the largest in the city, provide a minimum of 531 square feet. The hotel's acclaimed health facilities boast a stunning pool and the 14,000-square-foot **Peninsula Spa**, which takes up the top two floors of the hotel. And **Avenues ($$$$)** restaurant consistently rates among the best in Chicago. Afternoon tea is served in the soaring lobby as live string music drifts down from a tiny balcony that overlooks the room.

EXPENSIVE

Amalfi Hotel

$$$$ 215 rooms
20 W. Kinzie St., River North.
312-395-9000 or 877-262-5341.
www.amalfihotelchicago.com.

At the Amalfi, your well-appointed room is your sanctuary, complete with Egyptian cotton linens, a pillow-top mattress and multihead shower. The concierge is your "Experience Designer"; he or she is available to consult with you upon arrival regarding all the hip things you want to do while you're in the neighborhood, and can be summoned throughout your visit to assist with crises or answer questions. While the hotel lacks a dining room, complimentary continental breakfast is served on each floor, and food can be ordered in from **Harry Caray's** restaurant *(see p127)* across the street. **Keefers ($$$)**, on the first floor, serves splendid steaks and chops.

The Drake Hotel

$$$$ 537 rooms
140 E. Walton Pl., Magnificent Mile.
312-787-2200 or 800-445-7667.
www.thedrakehotel.com.

Since 1920, the Italian Renaissance-style limestone building at the north end of the Magnificent Mile has been *the* address for visiting celebrities. Antique solid-brass candelabras and the original mahogany ceiling inset with hand-painted tiles set the tone in the lobby. Rooms, some overlooking Lake Michigan, combine floral fabrics with dark woods. The old-fashioned (it opened in 1933)

The Drake Hotel

The Drake Hotel

but respected **Cape Cod Room ($$$$)** serves—what else?—seafood at lunch and dinner in a business-casual atmosphere. The Drake is now a Hilton property. High Tea in the lovely Palm Court is a must while you're in Chicago *(see p30)*.

The Fairmont Chicago

$$$$ 692 rooms
200 N. Columbus Dr., Loop.
312-565-8000 or 800-866-5577.
www.fairmont.com/chicago.

Rising just east of Millennium Park, the Fairmont has long provided a home away from home for political figures and celebrities. Spacious rooms are well appointed with soothing colors and contemporary style; you'll have your choice of city or lake views. Guests have access to the

Fairmont Chicago

Fairmont Hotels and Resorts

MUST STAY

luxurious Lakeshore Athletic Club next door, with its six floors of workout facilities, including a 110-foot-high climbing wall and an eight-lane pool. And for business travelers, there's a full-service business center on-site. Tea is served each afternoon in the Lobby Lounge. This is a great location for attending summer music festivals.

InterContinental Chicago

$$$$ 807 rooms
505 N. Michigan Ave., Magnificent Mile. 312-944-4100 or 800 628-2112. www.interconti.com.

InterContinental Chicago

This Mag Mile classic began life as a men's club in 1929 and still retains many of the club's original decorative embellishments *(see p28)*. Egyptian, Renaissance and Middle Eastern motifs ornament public spaces and ballrooms, giving the public areas a thoroughly exotic ambience, and lavish majolica tile sets off the hotel's celebrated junior Olympic-size swimming pool. South tower rooms are furnished in elegant Biedermeier style and have the best views; those in the north tower sport a more modern look. Dine on regional American dishes at **Zest ($$$)**, which has been remodeled with minimalist panache.

Lobby, James Chicago
James Hotel

James Chicago

$$$$ 297 rooms
55 E. Ontario St., Magnificent Mile. 312-337-1000 or 877-526-3755. www.jameshotels.com.

Once the site of the family-friendly Lenox Suites, the James Chicago has quickly become the must-stay locale for the young, hip and well-heeled. Swanky yet minimalist rooms scream understated luxury, while attentive service makes everyone feel like a celebrity. If you feel like a steakhouse splurge, try the equally-swanky **David Burke's Primehouse**, on the first floor. Burke is known for having his own cattle, including a stud named Prime.

The Raffaello Hotel

$$$$ 172 rooms
201 E. Delaware Pl., Magnificent Mile. 312-235-6312. www.chicago raffaello.com.

Rustic Old World charm emanates from the beamed ceilings and arched windows of this small hotel located east of Michigan Avenue. Less showy than other Michigan Avenue boutique properties, the the newly-renovated Raffaello claims to be the city's only luxury, all no smoking hotel. Rooms are

HOTELS

Trump International Hotel and Tower

Trump International Hotel and Tower

MUST STAY

simple but spacious, featuring one king or two double beds.

Trump International Hotel and Tower

$$$$ 339 rooms
401 N. Wabash Ave., Magnificent Mile. 877-458-7867. www.trump chicagohotel.com.

The name says it all. When Donald Trump puts his last name on a hotel, you know it is going to be expensive, but also packed with amenities. Rooms at the new Trump hotel have floor-to-ceiling windows, so you have excellent views of the Chicago River and the skyline. The rooms have full kitchens, although it is hard to resist the hotel's restaurants.

W Chicago Lakeshore

$$$$ 556 rooms
644 N. Lakeshore Dr., Gold Coast. 312-943-9200 or 888-625-5144. Also at 172 W. Adams St., Loop. www.starwoodhotels.com.

Overlooking the lakefront, W's "spectacular" rooms afford great views of Navy Pier and the lake beyond, while those dubbed

"wonderful" face the cityscape. With serenity in mind, the décor takes something of a Zen twist in its deep colors and strong lines. Rooms come equipped with electronic amenities including CD/DVD players, with a 24-hour CD library at your service.

Wheeler Mansion

$$$$ 11 rooms
2020 S. Calumet Ave., Near South Side. 312-945-2020. www.wheelermansion.com.

A stay here will give you a glimpse into life on Chicago's once-elegant Near South Side. Built in 1870, just a year before the Chicago Fire, this landmark is located in the **Prairie Avenue Historic District★**, not far from Glessner House *(see p74)*. Individual room decorations suggest a 19th century style, with dark wood trim, antique queen beds and marble baths, all private. The house is conveniently located for South Side activities, including conventions at McCormick Place, and is not far from the lakefront. Complimentary gourmet breakfast and parking are included with your reservation.

INEXPENSIVE

Affinia Chicago

$$$ 215 rooms
166 East Superior St., Magnificent Mile. 312-787-6000 or 800-367-7701. www.affinia.com.

Once the home of the Fitzpatrick Hotel, the Affinia Chicago brings another hip boutique hotel to the Mag Mile area. The luxury property includes a pillow menu, with six different options! The hotel's fish and chops restaurant, **C-House**, attracts lots of local buzz.

Denihan Hospitality Group

Guest Room, Affinia Chicago

Allerton Hotel Chicago

$$$ 443 rooms
701 N. Michigan Ave., Magnificent Mile. 312-440-1500. www.theallertonhotel.com.

The Allerton has served Chicago as a hotel since 1924, and a renovation has nicely restored its original polish inside and out. Guest rooms are outfitted with marble baths and glow with warm wood tones and a rich palette of wall and fabric colors. Check out the view from the top-floor fitness center. The famous Tip-Top-Tap that once occupied the 23rd floor has been moved to the second floor and transformed into **Taps on Two ($$$)** French bistro.

Conrad Chicago
Conrad Hotel

Conrad Chicago

$$$ 311 rooms
521 N. Rush St., Magnificent Mile. 312-645-1500. www.conrad hotels.com.

With Nordstrom—including Nordstrom Spa—and the entire North Bridge mall at your doorstep, the shopper staying at Conrad Chicago wants for nothing (you don't even need to go outside to reach the mall). Of course, the hotel is convenient to the entire Mag Mile, and its opulence is contemporary and understated with honey-tone woods, neutral colors and clean lines.

Hard Rock Hotel

$$$ 381 rooms
230 N. Michigan Ave., Loop. 312-345-1000. www.hardrock hotelchicago.com.

Smack dab between the Loop and the Mag Mile, this newish property has convenience and a lot more going for it. The jazzy Art Deco Carbide and Carbon building has been skillfully converted to accommodate this cool new hotel. Integrating the best of the old with a bit of new dazzle, including a moderate number of rock 'n' roll artifacts, the Hard Rock manages

HOTELS

Hard Rock Hotel

Hard Rock Hotel Chicago

boyantly decorated throughout, the hotel makes a fitting partner for the exuberant **House of Blues** restaurant/nightclub next door *(see p113)*. The rooms feature lots of high-tech perks. Located along the Chicago River in landmark Marina City, the complex also includes a 36-lane bowling alley, boat charters, a health club, a wine bar, and an upscale steakhouse.

a high degree of sophistication. Modern guest-room amenities include flat-screen TVs, DVD/CD 5-disc changers, free WiFi and dual-line phones. It's a convenient walk from here to the many attractions up and down Michigan Avenue, as well as east to the lakefront and along the river.

Hyatt Regency Chicago

$$$ 2,019 rooms
151 E. Wacker Dr., Loop.
312-565-1234. www.chicago
regency.hyatt.com.

If you're a Hyatt fan, welcome to the Mothership. This is the chain's largest property, and it's a behemoth. The glass-enclosed lobby, set about with greenery and fountains, can be something of an oasis, and the hotel's Big Bar sports the longest freestanding bar in North America, if such things matter. (As you might imagine, it serves everything BIG.) Its huge windows also offer good views looking north over the river. The hotel's location on East Wacker makes it convenient to destina-

Hotel 71

$$$ 454 rooms
71 E. Wacker Dr., Loop.
312-346-7100. www.hotel71.com.

Billing itself as an "urban hotel adventure," 71 has given a tired 1950s hotel an extreme makeover. Though the façade retains a dated look, the interior public spaces and rooms have bold, upbeat colors, animal prints and ultrasuede, and sleek furniture. Light sculptures add a chic touch. Rooms on the north side overlook the Chicago River.

Hotel Sax

$$$ 367 rooms
333 N. Dearborn St.,
River North. 312-245-0333.
www.hotelsaxchicago.com.

Forget English-manor style and French-country charm, the Hotel Sax aims to rock your world. Flam-

Hyatt Regency Chicago

Hyatt Hotels and Resorts

tions on both sides of the river, as well as Millennium Park and the lakefront. Chicago has several other Hyatt hotels as well.

Palmer House Hilton

$$$ 1,639 rooms
17 E. Monroe St., Loop.
312-726-7500 or 800-445-8667.
www.hiltonchicagosales.com.

Famous for its stunning hand-painted Beaux Arts ceiling, Empire Ballroom and lobby space, this Chicago fixture is dusting itself off with an interior renovation. The hotel's site on the corner of State Street in the Loop is convenient to shopping, dining, theater, Millennium Park and the Art Institute, making it a favorite among conventioneers and visitors interested in downtown attractions. The Palmer House features **Trader Vic's Restaurant ($$$)**, something of a historic attraction itself for its oh-so-1950s Polynesian umbrella drinks.

Silversmith Crowne Plaza

$$$ 143 Rooms
10 S. Wabash Ave., Loop.
312-372-7696 or 800-227-6963.
www.crowneplaza.com.

Tucked into Jeweler's Row just feet from the elevated tracks, the beautifully appointed Silversmith comes as an elegant surprise. Built in 1897 as a warren for jewelry makers, the National Historic Landmark was converted into a hotel and renovated in late 19th century Arts and Crafts style. Rich oak paneling, glazed terra-cotta and Stickley furnishings throughout make a nice change from both hotel modern and B&B flounce. Don't

be put off by the hotel's proximity to the elevated tracks; windows have been soundproofed. For extra quiet, however, ask for a room closer to the tenth floor.

Sofitel Chicago Water Tower

$$$ 415 rooms
20 E. Chestnut St., Magnificent Mile. 312-324-4000 or 800-763-4835. www.sofitel.com.

Sofitel Chicago Water Tower

Sofitel Chicago Water Tower

The talk of all the architectural circles, the dramatic upside-down exterior and slick, too-cool interior of the new Sofitel live up to the buzz. The techno-hip lobby employs decorative lighting and artwork to distinct advantage, and the rooms carry through with sophisticated contemporary European styling.

Sofitel's sleek brasserie, **Café des Architectes ($$$)**, serves seafood and other dishes accented with Mediterranean, Asian and Latin American flavors.

HOTELS

Classic Room, Swissôtel

Swissôtel

$$$ 632 rooms
*323 E. Wacker Dr., Loop.
312-565-0565 or 888-737-9477.
www.chicago.swissotel.com.*

Designed by prominent Chicago architect Harry Weese, the Swissôtel cuts a crisp and shimmering 43-story silhouette, its triangular shape wrapped entirely in glass. The property exudes a quiet elegance, and the best thing about its spacious, well-appointed rooms (besides the doorbells) is the magnificent view from every one. The Penthouse Health Club and Spa, one of the largest in a Chicago hotel, boasts all the necessities: lap pool, sauna, steam room and whirlpool. Swissôtel caters largely to corporate travelers, so its business amenities—meeting spaces, a business center, secretarial services and so on—are second to none. The hotel is undergoing a $64.5 million renovation meaning the meeting space will be ready in June 2009 and a brand new 54,000-square-foot ballroom will be completed toward the end of 2009.

Talbott Hotel

$$$ 147 rooms
20 E. Delaware Pl., Magnificent Mile. 312-944-4970 or 800-825-2688. www.talbotthotel.com.

Snug and intimate with an English fox-hunting theme, the tony Talbott features antiques and two fireplaces in its wood-paneled Victorian lobby. Guest rooms and suites, some with full kitchens, are simply but tastefully appointed in period reproductions. The hotel's overall tranquility transports guests far from the bustle of nearby Michigan Avenue, and the concierge can help with anything from procuring theater tickets to setting up a meeting. Guests here also enjoy nightly turndown service and complimentary access to the 72,000-square-foot Gold Coast Multiplex fitness facility.

The Whitehall Hotel

$$$ 221 rooms
105 E. Delaware Pl., Magnificent Mile. 312-944-6300 or 800 948-4255. www.thewhitehallhotel.com.

Just steps off the north end of Mag Mile (one block south of haute-couture shopping on Oak Street; see p103), this venerable inn is among the original small hotels in the city, serving an elite clientele since 1974. Today it retains its polish thanks to a renovation that has refreshed its English country-manor atmosphere. Light-filled rooms are done in neutral tones offset by dark period furnishings. The attentive staff provides personalized service, and small pets (under 30 pounds) are accepted.

BUDGET

Best Western Hawthorne Terrace

$$ 59 rooms
3434 N. Broadway, Lakeview.
773-244-3434 or 888-860-3400.
www.hawthorneterrace.com.

Nestled in a neighborhood on Chicago's North Side, the Hawthorne Terrace offers a charming boutique ambience convenient to Wrigley Field and the lakefront. Rooms have a vintage feel, with flowered wallpaper and bedspreads; many come equipped with whirlpool tubs, refrigerators and microwaves, and garden views. Enjoy a complimentary continental breakfast with your newspaper each morning. There's even a small workout room.

City Suites Hotel

$$ 45 Rooms
933 W. Belmont Ave., Lakeview.
773-404-3400 or 800-248-9108.
www.cityinns.com.

City Suites inhabits a neighborhood that bustles with street life day and night, crowded as it is with restaurants, bars, nightclubs and even a tattoo parlor. Most of the units in this Art Deco restoration are suites furnished with hide-a-beds and refrigerators, though some standard queen rooms are available for less. Unexpected amenities such as refrigerators, shaving/make-up mirrors and robes make City Suites a good bet for the price. The elevated train just west provides rapid transportation to downtown.

The Essex Inn

$$ 267 rooms
800 S. Michigan Ave., Grant Park.
312-939-2800 or 800-621-6909.
www.essexinn.com.

Though its rooms are basic, the Essex appeals for its good prices and convenient location along South Michigan Avenue. A recent renovation added a garden pool and fitness center on the fourth-floor rooftop. Across the street, Grant Park makes a lovely front yard, and the hotel is within walking distance of the Loop, Millennium Park, the lakefront and Art Institute.

Hotel Allegro Chicago

$$ 483 rooms
171 W. Randolph St., Loop.
312-236-0123 or 800-643-1500.
www.allegrochicago.com.

Bold colors and prints have transformed the North Loop theater district's 1926 Bismarck Hotel into a stylish Hollywood set. The lobby's fluted glass and oak-paneled walls are the backdrop for cobalt-blue velvet chaise lounges and red velour sofas. Guest rooms sport contemporary colors (pumpkin-colored walls and oversize

HOTELS

147

Queen Deluxe Room, Hotel Allegro

David Phelps/Kimpton Group

upholstered brown and cream headboards) and modern amenities (a sound system, a flat-screen TV and WiFi).

Traveling with your pet? Dogs and cats are welcome at Hotel Allegro, which even offers special packages for pets and their humans.

Hotel Burnham

$$ 122 rooms
1 W. Washington St., Loop.
312-782-1111 or 877-294-9712.
www.burnhamhotel.com.

Designed by Daniel Burnham's architectural firm in 1895, the

Hotel Burham in the Reliance Building

Kimpton Group

historic **Reliance Building★★** was restored in 1999 as the fanciful Hotel Burnham. Here original design elements, such as the mosaic floor and ornamental metal elevator grilles, blend with bold interior stylings, including royal-blue velvet headboards and matching cornices in the guest rooms. Conveniently located for shoppers, across from Marshall Field, the Burnham is also within walking distance of theaters, the Art Institute, Millennium Park and the lakefront. Enjoy American comfort food in the hotel's **Atwood Café ($$$)**.

Hotel Monaco

$$ 192 rooms
225 N. Wabash Ave., Loop.
312-960-8500 or 866-610-0081.
www.monaco-chicago.com.

Two blocks from the Loop or the Mag Mile, this boutique property was designed as the world traveler's 1930s Art Deco-style living room. In the oversize lobby, the registration desk is modeled after a classic steamer trunk. Guest rooms are done in dark woods and pistachio green in the French Deco

MUST STAY

Rock Star Suite,
Hotel Monaco

style. Whimsical amenities include an in-room pet goldfish on request and "tall" rooms with nine-foot beds and extra-high shower-heads. If you're traveling with your entourage, check out the Rock Star Suite; it has hosted the likes of James Taylor and Britney Spears. In a bit of a contrast, down-home all-American cooking—including a red-wine-glazed meatloaf "TV dinner"—is available next door at **South Water Kitchen ($$)**.

Majestic Hotel

$$ 53 rooms
528 Brompton Ave., Lakeview. 773-404-3499 or 800-727-5108. www.cityinns.com.

Going to a Cubs game? Located steps from Wrigley Field, as well as Lincoln Park and Belmont Harbor, this comfortable English-style inn is nicely situated for North Side activities. Of the 53 units, 22 are suites that include refrigerators, microwaves and wet bars. Amenities include robes, morning newspaper and a continental breakfast served in the lobby each morning. Prices dip considerably in the low season.

Millennium Knickerbocker Hotel

$$ 305 rooms
163 E. Walton Pl., Magnificent Mile. 312-751-8100 or 866-266-8086. www.millenniumhotels.com.

Transformed several times since its construction in 1927, the Knickerbocker underwent a hugely expensive, relatively recent renovation. Its distinctive cathedral-style windows and lit marquee welcome guests as they did in Prohibition-era Chicago, and the breathtaking, 5,000-square-foot Crystal Ballroom (now used for meetings and special events) still echoes with the sounds of the Jazz Age. Rooms are small but comfortable. The **Martini Bar** serves 44 varieties of its namesake against a musical backdrop of live jazz piano.

Seneca Hotel

$$ 160 rooms
200 E. Chestnut St., Magnificent Mile. 312-787-8900 or 800-800-6261. www.senecahotel.com.

Set in the shadow of the John Hancock Center, the venerable Seneca is a sturdy old residence hotel that offers travelers 160 rooms and suites with complete kitchens (including dishwashers) and comfortable rooms (100 additional rooms are reserved for residential guests). A stay here is a little like visiting grandmother, in all the good ways: nothing too fancy but homey, sensible and well situated. Just a block east of Michigan Avenue, the Seneca is within walking distance of the Museum of Contemporary Art and all the shops of Water Tower Place,

Sutton Place Hotel

both business and getaway travelers. Comfortable rooms are custom furnished with contemporary flair and a hint of Art Deco design; suites offer large living areas and wet bars. The marble baths are particularly nice here, with separate soaking tubs and showers. A full-service business center on the fourth floor offers everything from video-conferencing to document processing, and the sleek **Whiskey Bar** lounge is a perfect place to entertain clients.

The Tremont Hotel

$$ 130 rooms
100 E. Chestnut St. Magnificent Mile. 312-751-1900 or 800-621-8133. www.tremontchicago.com.

Another lodging in the English style, the Tremont is named for a "luxury" hotel that opened in 1838. Its cozy lobby, complete with a fireplace, welcomes guests with manor-house ambience; likewise the bright rooms and suites. The Tremont House next door offers 12 furnished suites with kitchens for those traveling with families or desiring a longer stay. Named for

the Mag Mile and Oak Street. While it offers no dining facilities of its own, a deli, wine bar and the **Saloon Steakhouse** *(see p129)* are located in the building, along with a full-service salon and spa.

Sutton Place Hotel

$$ 246 rooms
21 E. Bellevue Pl., Magnificent Mile. 312-266-2100 or 866-378-8866. www.suttonplace.com.

Stylish and elegant, the modern 23-story Sutton Place caters to

The Tremont Hotel

the infamous former coach of "Da Bears," **Mike Ditka's ($$$)** restaurant is located in the hotel, with downstairs dining (think steaks and chops) and a cigar bar on the second level.

The Willows Hotel

$$ 55 rooms
555 W. Surf St., Lincoln Park. 773-528-8400 or 800-727-3108. www.cityinns.com.

The Willows occupies a vintage 1920s building just off busy Broadway. Renovated in 19th century French country style, the lobby is pretty in tones of pink and peach. Though bathrooms are small, the rooms are restful, done in a soft pastel palette. Not far away are Diversey Harbor, the Notebaert Nature Museum and Lincoln Park Zoo, along with shopping and dining on Broadway and surrounding blocks. Ask about the seasonal package deals.

Wooded Isle Suites

$$ 13 rooms
5750 S. Stony Island Ave., South Side. 773-288-5578 or 800-290-6844. www.woodedisle.com.

If you're planning to spend much of your visit around Hyde Park, these converted apartments might be most convenient for you. Located in a typical Chicago courtyard building, the 13 suites include one-bedroom apartments that sleep four or studios that sleep two in a Murphy bed. Separate eat-in kitchens add extra convenience. Steps away you'll find the University of Chicago, the Museum of Science and Industry and the beach. McCormick Place,

the Museum Campus and the Loop are just a short hop away by car or public transportation.

Red Roof Inn

$ 208 rooms
162 E. Ontario St., Magnificent Mile. 312-787-3580 or 800-733-7663. www.redroof.com.

Who'd have guessed it? A reasonably priced, perfectly suitable hotel just off the Mag Mile in one of Chicago's hottest neighborhoods? Even if the room does remind you of your last road trip, your checkbook will be ahead of the game.

Staying in Oak Park and Evanston

The Carleton of Oak Park Hotel and Motor Inn

$$ 154 rooms
1110 Pleasant St., Oak Park. 708-848-5000 or 888-227-5386. www.carletonhotel.com.

Opened in 1928 as Oak Park's "high-class hotel," the Carleton offers pleasant accommodations convenient to downtown Oak Park and about 20 minutes from the Loop via the nearby elevated train.

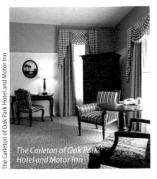

The Carleton of Oak Park Hotel and Motor Inn

The Carleton of Oak Park Hotel and Motor Inn

The Homestead

Motor-inn rooms are slightly less in cost. Most rooms have microwaves and refrigerators.

The Homestead

$$ 90 rooms
1625 Hinman Ave., Evanston. 847-475-3300. www.thehomestead.net.

This colonial-style manse was built in 1928 as a genteel hotel "in a wonderful location." It still caters to both overnighters and extended-stay guests with single rooms, studios, and one- and two-bedroom apartments. Reservations include a continental breakfast and garage parking, and the rooms are simple but comfortable. The lakefront, downtown Evanston and the Northwestern University campus are all within walking distance, as are plenty of good places to eat.

Hotel Orrington

$$ 269 rooms
1710 Orrington Ave., Evanston. 847-866-8700 or 888-677-4648. www.hotelorrington.com.

After a relatively recent $32 million renovation, the 1923 Orrington is freshly reopened. Retaining its lovely 1920s feel, the updated hotel now sports a fresh interior design and added amenities. All of its rooms, suites, banquet facilities and common areas have been refurbished and provisioned to please both vacation and business travelers and to attract meetings and private gatherings. Located adjacent to Northwestern University and around the corner from Evanston's shopping and dining district, the Orrington is well placed for Evanston visitors.

The Write Inn

$ 111 rooms
211 N. Oak Park Ave., Oak Park. 708-383-4800. www.writeinn.com.

This suburban inn is located along a shady stretch of residential street just steps from Oak Park's historic attractions and trains to the Loop. It sits across the street from the Hemingway Museum, and just north you'll find Hemingway's Birthplace. Decorated with 1920s period antiques, rooms range from small chambers outfitted with Murphy beds to larger rooms featuring sitting areas, whirlpool tubs and kitchenettes.

HOTELS BY THEME

Looking for good business hotels in Chicago? Want to bring Fido along? In the preceding pages, we've organized the properties by price category, so below we've broken them out by theme to help you plan your trip. *Hotels listed below are located in Chicago unless otherwise noted.*

Close to Wrigley Field
Best Western Hawthorne
   Terrace *(p147)*
Majestic Hotel *(p149)*

Easy on the Budget
The Carleton of Oak Park Hotel
   and Motor Inn (Oak Park) *(p151)*
The Essex Inn *(p147)*
Red Roof Inn *(p151)*
The Write Inn (Oak Park) *(p152)*

For Business Travelers
The Fairmont Chicago *(p140)*
Four Seasons *(p139)*
Hard Rock Hotel *(p143)*
Hyatt Regency Chicago *(p144)*
Palmer House Hilton *(p145)*
Sofitel Chicago Water Tower *(p145)*
Swissôtel *(p146)*
Sutton Place Hotel *(p150)*

For Families
James Chicago *(p141)*
City Suites Hotel *(p147)*
Seneca Hotel *(p149)*
The Tremont Hotel *(p150)*
Wooded Isle Suites *(p151)*

Hippest Décor
Hard Rock Hotel *(p143)*
Hotel Allegro Chicago *(p147)*
Hotel Monaco *(p148)*
Hotel 71 *(p144)*
Sofitel Chicago Water Tower *(p145)*

Hotels with History
The Drake Hotel *(p140)*
The Homestead (Evanston) *(p152)*
Hotel Burnham *(p148)*
Hotel Orrington *(p151)*

InterContinental Chicago *(p141)*
Palmer House Hilton *(p145)*
Silversmith Crowne Plaza *(p145)*
Wheeler Mansion *(p142)*
The Willows Hotel *(p151)*

Near Mag Mile Shopping
Allerton Hotel Chicago *(p143)*
James Chicago *(p141)*
The Drake Hotel *(p140)*
Four Seasons Hotel *(p139)*
InterContinental Chicago *(p141)*
The Peninsula Chicago *(p139)*
Red Roof Inn *(p151)*
Seneca Hotel *(p149)*
Sofitel Chicago Water Tower *(p145)*
Sutton Place Hotel *(p150)*
Talbott Hotel *(p146)*
The Tremont Hotel *(p150)*
The Whitehall Hotel *(p146)*

Pet-Friendly Hotels
Hotel Allegro Chicago *(p147)*
Hotel Monaco *(p148)*
Sofitel Chicago Water Tower *(p145)*
W Chicago Lakeshore *(p142)*

Posh Places
Amalfi Hotel *(p140)*
The Drake Hotel *(p140)*
The Fairmont Chicago *(p140)*
Four Seasons Hotel *(p139)*
InterContinental Chicago *(p141)*
The Peninsula Chicago *(p139)*

Spa Experiences
The Fairmont Chicago *(p140)*
Four Seasons Hotel *(p139)*
The Peninsula Chicago *(p139)*
Swissôtel *(p146)*

HOTELS

CHICAGO

The following abbreviations may appear in this Index: NHS National Historic Site; NM National Monument; NMem National Memorial; NP National Park; NHP National Historical Park; NRA National Recreational Area; NWR National Wildlife Refuge; SP State Park; SHP State Historical Park; SHS State Historic Site.

A

AARP 17
Accessibility 16
Accommodations, *see Hotels* 17
Acorn Express 83
Adler, Max 52
Adler Planetarium 51
Airports 13
Airport Transfers 13
Alfred Caldwell Lily Pool 66
American Girl Place 100
American Football 19
Andersonville 33
Area Codes 17
Art Institute of Chicago 44, 93
   American Art 46
   Asian Art 46
   European Decorative Arts 46
   European Painting and
      Sculpture 45
   19th century European
      Painting 46
   Modern Wing, The 46
Astor Street 32
Auditorium Building 22

B

Bahá'í House of Worship 81
Bailly Homestead and Chellberg
   Farm and Trail (IN) 86
Ballet 121
Baseball 19
Basketball 19
Beaches 91
"Big John" 38, 40
Biograph Theater 90, 123
Bootleggers 21

Bridgeport, Bronzeville and
Chinatown 36
   Blues Heaven 36
   Illinois Institute of
      Technology (IIT) 36
   US Cellular Field 36
Brookfield Zoo 97
Buckingham Fountain 64
Bucktown and Wicker Park 35
   Flat Iron Arts Building 35
Bus 14

C

Calendar of Events 10
Capone, Al 21
Car 14
Car Rental 16
Carr Memorial Chapel 36
Chicago Botanic Garden 81
Chicago Children's Museum 97
Chicago Cultural Center 23
Chicago Greeters 15
Chicago History Museum 54
Chicago School of Architecture 24
Chicago Water Tower and
   Pumping Station 42
Chinese-American Museum
   of Chicago 55
Climate 12
Comedy Clubs
   ComedySportz 118
   ImprovOlympic 118
   Second City, The 118
   Zanies 118
ComedySportz4Kidz 101
Communications 17
Currency 19
Customs 13

INDEX

154

D

Daley, Richard J. 21
Disabilities, Travelers with 16
  AccessNotes 17
  SATH 16
  Mayor's Office for People with
    Disabilities 16
  National Park Service 16
Discount Passes 18
  $5 Weekend Pass 18
  CityPass 18
  GoChicago Card 18
  Metra 10-Ticket Ride 18
Drake Hotel, The 30, 140
Driving 14
DuSable Museum of African
  American History 55

E

Electricity 18
Elijah Muhammad House 37
Emergency Numbers 18
Entry Requirements 13
Ernest Hemingway Birthplace 80
ESPN Zone 101
Excursions 78

F

Festivals 10, 90
  ArtChicago 10
  Bud Billiken Day Parade 11
  Celtic Fest Chicago 11
  Chicago Air & Water Show 11
  Chicago Blues Festival 10
  Chicago Gospel Festival 10
  Chicago Flower and Garden
    Show 10
  Chicago Jazz Festival 11
  Chicago Marathon 11
  Chicago Summer
    Neighborhood Festivals 10
  Chinese New Year Parade 10
  Day of the Dead (Dia de los
    Muertos) 11, 58
  Grant Park Music Festival 11
  International Antiques Fair 10
  Mag Mile Lights Festival 11, 30

Major League Baseball
    Opening Day 10
  Mayor Daley's Kids and Kites'
    Festival 10
  Old Town Art Fair 10
  Ravinia Festival 10, 123
  St. Patrick's Day Parade 10
  Taste of Chicago 10
  Viva! Chicago Latin Music
    Festival 11
  Winter Wonder Fest 11
  World Music Festival 11
Field Museum of Natural
  History 93
Finnegan's Ice Cream Parlor 96
Forest Avenue 79
Frank Lloyd Wright Home
  and Studio 79

G

Garfield Park Conservatory 67
Gold Coast 32
  Charnley-Persky House 32
Golf 92
Graceland Cemetery 70
Grant Park 63
Great Chicago Fire 20

H

Hancock Observatory, The 39
Henry B. Clarke House 74
Historic Sites 70
Hostels 17
Hotel Reservation Services 17
Hotels
  Amalfi Hotel 140
  Affinia Chicago 143
  Allerton Hotel Chicago 143
  Best Western Hawthorne
    Terrace 147
  Carleton of Oak Park Hotel
    and Motor Inn 151
  City Suites Hotel 147
  Conrad Chicago 143
  Drake Hotel, The 140
  Essex Inn, The 147
  Fairmont Chicago 140

Four Seasons Hotel 139
Hard Rock Hotel 143
Homestead, The 152
Hotel 71 144
Hotel Sax 144
Hotel Allegro Chicago 147
Hotel Burnham 27, 148
Hotel Monaco 148
Hotel Orrington 152
Hyatt Regency Chicago 144
InterContinental Chicago 141
James Chicago 141
Majestic Hotel 149
Millennium Knickerbocker
   Hotel 149
Palmer House Hilton 145
Peninsula Chicago, The 139
Raffaello Hotel, The 141
Red Roof Inn 151
Seneca Hotel 149
Silversmith Crowne Plaza 145
Sofitel Chicago Water
   Tower 145
Sutton Place Hotel 150
Swissôtel 146
Talbott Hotel 146
Tremont Hotel, The 150
Trump International Hotel
   and Tower 142
Willows Hotel, The 151
W Chicago Lakeshore 142
Wheeler Mansion 142
Whitehall Hotel, The 146
Wooded Isle Suites 151
Write Inn, The 152
Hutchinson Street District 72
Hyde Park 37

I

Ice skating 92
Illinois & Michigan Canal National
   Heritage Corridor 83
Indiana Dunes National
   Lakeshore 85
Indiana Dunes SP 85
InterContinental Chicago 28
International Museum of

Surgical Science 56
International Visitors 13
Internet 17
Intuit: The Center for Intuitive
   and Outsider Art 56

J

Jackson Park 68
Jane Addams Hull-House
   Museum 72
Jenney, William Le Baron 25
John Hancock Center 38
John Hancock Tower 40
John Jacob Glessner House 74

K

Kids' Activities 93
   American Girl Place 100
   Art Institute of Chicago 93
   Brookfield Zoo 97
   Chicago Children's
      Museum 97
   Children's Museum of
      Immigration 101
   ComedySportz4Kidz 101
   ESPN Zone 101
   Field Museum of Natural
      History 93
   Lincoln Park Zoo 99
   Museum of Science and
      Industry 48, 95
   Navy Pier 97
   Pritzker Family Children's
      Zoo 99
   Theater for Kids 98

L

Lake Michigan 40
Lakeview 37
Landmarks 38
Leather Archives and Museum 57
Lincoln Park 65
Lincoln Park Conservatory 67
Lincoln Park/DePaul 66
Lincoln Park Zoo 99
Lincoln Square 33
   Sulzer Regional Library 34

Little Saigon 33
Lloyd Wright, Frank 71
Lockport 83
Lookingglass Theatre 43
Loop, The, *see The Loop* 22

M

Magnificent Mile 27
  Fourth Presbyterian Church 28
  InterContinental Chicago 28
  Oak Street 30
  Tribune Tower 28
  Wrigley Building 27
Marina City 31
Marquette Building 40
McCormick Tribune Bridgehouse
  and Chicago River Museum 76
McCormick Tribune
  Campus Center 36
McCormick Tribune
  Freedom Museum 57
Mies van der Rohe, Ludwig 24, 36
Millennium Park 61, 91
  BP Bridge 62
  Cloud Gate 62
  Crown Fountain 63
  Jay Pritzker Pavilion 61
  Lurie Garden 63
  Museum Campus 64
Money 19
Mount Baldy 86
Museums 44
  Children's Museum of
    Immigration 101
  Chicago Children's Museum 97
  Chicago History Museum 54
  Chinese-American Museum
    of Chicago 55
  DuSable Museum of African
    American History 55
  Field Museum of Natural
    History 46, 93
  International Museum of
    Surgical Science 56
  Jane Addams Hull-House
    Museum 72

Leather Archives and
  Museum 57
McCormick Tribune Bridge-
  house and Chicago River
  Museum 76
McCormick Tribune Freedom
  Museum 57
Mitchell Museum of the
  American Indian 57
Morton Arboretum 82
Museum of
  Contemporary Art 54
Museum of Contemporary
  Photography 57
Museum of Holography 58
Museum of Science and
  Industry 48, 95
National Museum of
  Mexican Art 58
Peggy Notebaert Nature
  Museum 59
Polish Museum of America 60
Richard H. Driehaus
  Museum 77
Smart Museum of Art 55
Smith Museum of Stained-
  Glass Windows 60
Swedish-American Museum
  and Children's Museum of
  Immigration 101, 104
Spertus Museum 60
Music and Dance 121

N

860-880 North Lake
  Shore Drive 30
National American Italian Sports
  Hall of Fame 58
National Museum of
  Mexican Art 58
Navy Pier 15, 87, 97
Neighborhoods 22
  Andersonville 33
  Bridgeport, Bronzeville and
    Chinatown 36
  Bucktown and Wicker Park 35

Gold Coast 32
Hyde Park 37
Lakeview 37
Lincoln Square 33
Little Saigon 33
Loop, The, see The Loop 22
Magnificent Mile 27
Old Town 34
Pilsen 35
River North 31
Newberry Library 31
Newspapers 18
Nightlife
    Andy's Jazz Club 114
    B.L.U.E.S. 113
    Bin 36 117
    Blue Chicago 113
    Buddy Guy's Legends 113
    Cotton Club 114
    Double Door 116
    Empty Bottle 116
    Enclave 116
    Eno Wine Bar 117
    Excalibur 116
    Funky Buddha Lounge 116
    Green Dolphin Street 114
    Green Mill Jazz Club 114
    House of Blues 113
    Jimmy's Woodlawn Tap 116
    Joe Segal's Jazz Showcase 115
    Kingston Mines 114
    Liar's Club 116
    Lumen 116
    Metro 117
    New Checkerboard Lounge
        for Blues 'n' Jazz 115
    Paramount Room 117
    Pops for Champagne 115
    Velvet Lounge, The 115
    Violet Hour, The 117
North Shore 80

O
Oak Park 78
Oak Street Beach 91
Old Town 34
    Menomonee Street 34

Old Town Art Fair 34
Opening Hours 19
Opera 122
Oriental Institute 53
Ottawa 85

P
Parks and Gardens 61
Passports 13
Peggy Notebaert Nature
    Museum 59
Performing Arts 119
Pilsen 35
Pioneer Settlement (Lockport) 84
Pizzas 101
"Pleasant Home" (OP) 80
Polish Museum of America 60
Prairie Avenue Historic District 73
Public Transportation 15
    Bus 14
    Chicago Transit
        Authority (CTA) 13
    Elevated Commuter
        Rail Line 15
    Greyhound 14
    Navy Pier Trolley 15
    Shoreline Sightseeing 16
    Subway 15
    Taxi 16
    Train 14
    Water Taxis 16
Pullman Historic District 74

R
Ravinia Music Festival 123
Reliance Building 27
Restaurants
    17 West at the Berghoff 130
    Andies 130
    Ann Sather 132
    avec 130
    Arun's 124
    Big Shoulders 53
    Billy Goat Tavern 42
    Bistro 110 126
    Blackbird 126

Brasserie Jo 126
Breakfast Spots 138
Café Ba-Ba-Reeba! 131
Café Brauer 66
Café le Coq 136
Campagnola 136
Charlie Trotter's 124
Chef's Station 136
Chicago Pizza and Oven
    Grinder 132
Club Lucky 131
Custom House 127
Davis Street Fishmarket 136
Dixie Kitchen 137
Ed Debevic's 133
Erwin 131
Everest 124
Gino's East 131
Gold Coast Dogs 133
Green Door Tavern 133
Green Zebra 127
Half Shell 133
Harry Caray's 127
Healthy Food 134
Heaven on Seven 132
Herna's Kitchen 134
Hemmingway's Bistro 137
L20 125
Lou Mitchell's 134
Mr. Beef 134
North Pond 55
Petersen's Ice Cream Parlor
    and Sweet Shoppe 137
Pizzeria Due 101
Pizzeria Uno 101
Puck's 54
Rhapsody 128
Russian Tea Time 128
Saloon Steakhouse 129
Signature Room at the 95th 38
Spiaggia 125
Tapas Barcelona 136
The Pump Room 128
The Third Coast 135
Tizi Melloul 129
Topolobampo 129

Tru 125
Twin Anchors Restaurant
    Tavern 135
Union Pizzeria 137
Viet Bistro 135
Wishbone 135
Wow Bao 135
Richard H. Driehaus Museum 77
Richard J. Daley Center 25
River North 31
River North Gallery District 31
Robie House 71
Rookery 24
Rosehill 70

S
S.R Crown Hall 36
Sculpture 23
Sears Tower 39, 40
Senior Citizens 17
Shedd Aquarium 49, 94
    Amazon Rising: Seasons of
        the River 51
    Caribbean Reef 51
    Oceanarium 50
    Wild Reef 50
Shopping 19, 102
    Hyde Park 109
    Magnificent Mile 102
        Mag Mile Malls 102
    Merchandise Mart 24, 106
    New Maxwell Street Market 103
    Outlet Malls 109
    River North Galleries 107
    South Loop 108
    West Loop Galleries 108
Skydeck 43
Skyscrapers 25
Skywalk, Hancock Observatory 39
Smoking 19
Spas 110-112
Spectator Sports 19
Spertus Museum 60
Stephen A. Douglas Tomb
    and Memorial 77
Streeterville 30

T

Telephones 17
Theater 119-123
The Loop 22
   Auditorium Building 22
   Chicago Board of Trade
      Building 25
   Chicago Cultural Center 23
   Chicago School of
      Architecture 24
   Federal Center 24
   Former Location of Carson Pirie
      Scott & Company 23
   James R. Thompson Center 24
   Macy's State St. 26
   Richard J. Daley Center 25
   State Street 26
Time 19
Tipping 19
Tours
   Architecture Foundation
      Tours 32
   Ghost Tours 90
   Neighborhood Tours 90
   River Tours 42
   Untouchable Tours 90
Train 14
Travelers with Disabilities 16

U

Unity Temple 79
US Cellular Field 36
University of Chicago 53

V

Visas 13
Visitor Information Centers 12

W

Weather 12
Websites 12
West Beach Area 86
World's Columbian
   Exposition 21, 67
Wright, Frank Lloyd 79
Wrigley Field 43, 89

Z

Zoos 97, 99

List of Maps

Principal Sights: The Loop
inside front cover
Chicago Rapid Transit System
inside back cover
Magnificent Mile *28-29*

Central Chicago *41*
Greater Chicago *69*
Oak Park *81*

INDEX